I Testify: Seven Days of Healing

by Rochelle Washington

PUBLISHED BY: Speakwise Enterprise

PRODUCED BY: Nurisha Liggins for GLOW
Publications

I Testify: Seven Days of Healing
Copyright © 2017 by Rochelle Washington

ISBN: 978-0692915974

First Printing July 2017

Cover Design by Gannon Crutcher

Table of Contents

Dedication & Thank You

I dedicate this book to all the victims and survivors that have experienced child sexual abuse and the aftermath that goes along with it.

I want to thank God for a gift called life. I thank Him for being there for me during the darkest moments when I thought that no one cared about me. I want to thank my maternal grandmother for taking on the responsibility to raise me as best as she could. I want to thank my parents (RIH daddy) for being that chosen couple to get me to this earth to become this unique individual. A special thanks to my mother. I want to thank my mother for all that she endured known and unknown to help assist in my life's journey. And for the many that had a hand in raising me, I say thank you because I am an example of it takes a village!

I want to thank my children for always being that positive support throughout the years and putting up with a parent that was trying to find her way before and after each of their existence. I want to thank my legacy, my three grandsons, for giving me the drive to complete and share this project. I send a special thanks to each of you and the position that you held as I transitioned from child, young adult, to adult. May God bless each of you!

The events in this book is based on a true story.

Introduction

"Do you swear, to tell the truth, the whole truth and nothing but the truth?" How many times in a day do you think that this phrase is repeated throughout our system? I am speaking of the United States Justice System. I never got a chance to testify in a court of law as to what really happened to spin my childhood out of orbit, and why I respond the way that I do to certain situations. Before the trial begins, I will say that this is my life according to what happened to me. My intent is not to hurt or bring shame to the people that were involved in my upbringing, but to help heal someone by finally telling my story.

We all need to experience a spiritual, emotional, and physical healing from time to time. Wounds especially in our physical and emotional beings can often result in a generational curse that has been inherited and passed down from one generation to another.

It is important that we bear joyful witness to a forward movement of love, life and prosperity in our lives; and to do so I have learned that speaking the truth and forgiving my perpetrators was the solution to my healing process.

I pray a prayer of healing to any and all who are or

were victims of any circumstance that stunted your growth or threw you off-task according to God's original plans for your life. I not only pray this for my family, but the many families that are going to be touched throughout the pages of this book. May God keep you and bless every reader continuously.

Day One:
"Down Memory Lane"

"Well, Judge, as early as I can remember the strange and inappropriate things began to happen to me when I was about three years old. I can remember when my grandfather would take me under the bridge to drink booze with him and his fellows. Even at that time, we were High Cappin', Ballin as the youngsta's say it now. I remember him driving a white luxury car with red leather interior seats and our favorite song blasting on the radio, "Our Love" by Natalie Cole. Yes, I knew some of the words, but I didn't know exactly why we were singing them under the bridge. Remember, I was just a toddler.

One thing was for certain; my grandmother would always fuss at me later as if I knew better than to drink beer. I would sometimes get it from her, a spanking that is. Heck, I was taught to get my drink on at an early age. And no, I did not know better than to drink whatever was given to me.

If I could give a synopsis of my maternal grandmother, it would definitely start with church and end with church. My grandmother is the best, and I know that she did her best at raising me. I will forever be grateful that she decided to take on the responsibility of *grandmother* when she had so many other options of a forty-year old woman.

I want to set the record straight about who she is and what she means to me. I would not be the woman I am today if it were not for her taking me in as a baby and taking care of me as if I were one of her own children.

Now, about the fellow who was dubbed *"The Meanest Man in the World,"* at least the way my uncles tell it. He was the 'stepfather from hell,' and he dealt my mom and me a brutal hand. I did not remember everything that my family went through with him, but I can certainly remember the hard work that he handed to them, and even to me.

My job was to walk around in my grandmother's vegetable garden and to ride on the riding lawn mower. It was my job to explore what was planted and pick the vegetables as best as I could. As far as the riding on the mower, I believe it was a ploy to keep me from getting in the way and slowing down the production of everyone else. My job was not all that bad. When I was not riding and walking, he would mock me and make whiny faces to get me to stop crying. But the mark that he left in my life was the start of what I believed to be as an eternal cry.

He was a man of many faces and the one that I would hear about most often was his drunken face. They said when this man had too much to drink, he was *hellacious.* How does he relate to my experience, you may wonder? He was the first predator in a series of predators that I can remember in my life. It is usually the ones that you trust the most or that someone entrusted to take care of you that will do you the most damage, if not careful. When he would send me to "jail" for misbehaving, he in turn would sometimes step out of bounds and begin to "misbehave" worse than I had. (By the way, "jail" was the space in between the footrest of the recliner once it was extended.)

One incident led to many more similar occurrences in my life. I have always wondered how a person could find pleasure from a child when there are able-bodied adults willing to take on a sexual encounter. This has always puzzled me.

I can remember on a couple of occasions him sending me to "jail" and taking the opportunity to feel on me in inappropriate areas. It is sad, but it is true. Some may ask, 'how can you remember things which occurred at such a young age?' I would think that a three-year-old would have been expected to not remember as much as I have, but I did. I would leave the brilliancy of the human mind to the *Almighty Creator* himself. Our memory holds on to many experiences, whether good or bad. Some of these memories are suppressed until the day comes that you have to talk about them. This is exactly what happened to me. Events in my memory bank resurfaced during various therapy sessions where I had to revisit my past hurts. It amazes me how during therapy sessions I would have moments when I would recall certain things that happened to me. Then there were times when I drew a complete blank, and could not remember anything.

Nevertheless, I was the victim of *someone else's* wicked fantasy. *Someone* that was believed to have my best interest in mind, but only had self-gratification in mind.

The time spent in "jail" was the beginning of my experience with men abusing and misusing me, from infancy to young adulthood. Here I was, a young victim in the presence of those who thought that I was being cared for, but little did they know, abuse was taking place right behind their back...in some cases literally behind their back! He was slick with his approach, because "a feel" on a toddler would easily go unnoticed by others in the household. Only I, *The Warden* and God could remember the horrific exchanges of pure innocence and the emotional disturbance of a selfish and reckless individual. Oh, yes. I definitely remember. How could I forget? I was *the victim.*

"The Warden," my maternal grandmother's second husband is deceased, and has been for some years now. When I heard the news I could not bring myself to shed *not even one tear*. The grief I felt was temporary because of all of the hurt and pain this one man caused to our family. His death was meaningless to me because his mishandling of me became one of the many reasons that I embarked on a journey of mental rampage, wanting to kill *every* man who took advantage of me in a sexual manner. I like to think of them as *premeditated murders that never happened.*

As time went on during my journey, the plot of my plan was thickening in my head but I did not have the guts to carry it out. While there was only a handful of men that I had planned to carry out my mental plot, I would later come to realize that God had a different plan altogether. I realized that my way of getting back at them would not result in violence, but in a manner that would be surprising to all, including me."

"Out of the Mouth of a Babe"

Let us fast forward to some *good* memories from my childhood. There were times when I enjoyed what most children enjoyed...playing and being a child. There were moments when some parts of my elementary school days were joyous and special. My recollection of events that occurred during my elementary years is fairly decent, primarily because I considered these years as "the fun times." This period of my life was not as stressful in comparison to the impending trauma that was to come. I could remember some events quite well.

From my first childhood boyfriend in kindergarten, to my spelling bee in the sixth grade, these were the normal times for me. After my sixth grade year, I formed a mental block that caused me to remember certain events, but not as detailed as before. (I will elaborate on this a little later in the book). The trauma in my earlier years robbed me from having normal teenage girl experiences. I never had the chance to share "girl-talk" like most young girls do. You know, the talk when you visit one another's house and you openly admit to coming close to sex or trying to figure out what sex really means. Unfortunately, I was robbed of that special moment. The thief came into my life and took what was special and made it a nightmare.

Sad to say, the day came when I had the experience of seeing my first naked man. If my memory serves me correctly, I was almost eleven years old when this happened. It wasn't because I was being "womanish" or anything like that. The moment was very awkward, yet the word awkward doesn't best accurately describe what was being forced upon me.

The "Naked Man"

I was getting ready to go to a local wrestling event at Dallas' Reunion Arena; the building with the geodesic dome on top. This was one of those "Battle Royals" where all of the head honchos back in the day such as the Von Erich's, Kabuki the Wrestler, Andre the Giant, Kamala, and Rick Flair were the professional wrestling headliners. Wrestling and boxing were of the many sports I liked as a child. I was excited about the wrestling event, and also excited because this was my dad's weekend to have me over at his house. This was my time to spend with him and wife number three (we will reference her as "Three").

I had spent time with him and "Three" many times before, and I actually liked her. She was not the typical mean step-mother, although she had to put up with a lot of my dad's crap. I only heard about the things that my mom had to put up with concerning him, and I vaguely remember one incident as a toddler, but everything else I witnessed with my own eyes.

I knew my mother went through hell with him because his attitude was jacked up back then. He was very mean, and "mean" is a nice way of putting it. From what I understood, he physically abused my mom and cheated on her. I witnessed him continue this behavior with wives number "Two" through "Four." You can imagine the impact this left on me, the oldest daughter, witnessing this pattern of behavior at such impressionable ages.

While I was very excited about going to this wrestling event, I knew it would be in my best interest to settle down for a nap so that I could be alert for all of the ringside action. Speaking of action, I woke up to *unexpected* action. I woke up to this "naked man" standing over me, rubbing his huge hands on my breast and vagina. I was afraid, and now that I was awake so was he.

The fear seemed to paralyze me and blind me to my surroundings. The only thing I could see and feel was this grown man on top of my young body and a mattress beneath me. His hands and advances didn't lead to the real deal, sexual intercourse, but it was leading up to it. With his eyes intent on my reactions or lack thereof, he began suggesting another "session" by letting me know that he can make me "feel good." I could only assume that he was suggesting the *real deal*, or sex. I was so confused and did not know what to say but 'okay.' Now, before you start incriminating me, you must remember that I have seen this "naked man" slap three of his wives, cuss them out and physically assault them. As you can imagine, I was afraid!

Yes, I knew what sex was, or should I say I thought I knew what it was because of what I saw on television. I was confused because I wasn't quite sure if *this* was sex. I was being fondled, and because my undergarments were removed and what I was feeling wasn't right, quite naturally, I thought it was sex. I was confused because this was the same man that had given birth to me. I knew that sex was a forbidden subject, and not quite sure as to why I was introduced to this adult type of interaction from a person that I was taught to trust. I didn't tell anyone because I was told not to, and besides that, I was afraid of what could happen to me.

The household I was raised in seemed to be just about as normal as that of other folks. I was raised under a roof of a single mother and grandmother. My grandmother had two jobs and sometimes three if you included the weekend gigs. In between the jobs she was an avid church goer. Her focus was trying to make it in the world and raise her family. Our family was not as affectionate as some other families. We didn't do the hug and kiss thing, but each member of the family, including myself, was confident that we were loved. Love was not verbally expressed, but we all carried a knowing that we were not just bonded by blood, but by love and care for one another.

Because our household was not a place where we naturally expressed our feelings, the thought of telling my mother or grandmother what was going on never entered my mind. She would have been the last person I would have told about what was going on with me. Somewhere deep inside I felt as if my grandmother would have blamed me for what happened. I could actually hear a voice scolding me in my mind saying, "you know better than that."

"Let's Talk About Sex"

Sex was not a topic for discussion in my household. When my mother and grandmother felt as though I should know about "the birds and the bees," they decided to give me *"Life Cycle"* books to teach me about the female and male anatomy. Hell, everything else was a live and learn situation. I had to attend the school of hard knocks to figure the rest out. It was unfortunate for me that I did not learn the value and pleasure of intimacy, because it was not introduced to me in the proper way. The only way that I could escape from it all was to do well in school and pretend that everything in my little life was normal.

If *"Life Cycle"* was the choice way to teach me what I needed to know to avoid a much needed conversation, then *"Life Cycle"* it was. I assume that my mother and grandmother expected me to read my book and get the gist of sex because my mother only sat down with me once or twice to see if I was reading it. Child, please! When you are as developed as I was; with a butt, breast and thighs, those books were a day late and a dollar short. A straight-street conversation would have been enough to catch me up-to-date. You know what I mean – straight from the hood with a little realness to it. That's what a girl like me needed. I went on and never said anything about my daddy touching me the first time.

Time went on and for a while he didn't try anything else, but I didn't know how to feel about his distance from me or the incident that happened. As the days and weeks passed my thoughts tended to stay right where the event occurred. "Was this man trying to be my boyfriend?" I would think to myself.

No matter how much I reasoned with my thoughts, I could never figure it all out. I became even more confused with all that was going on, because I just couldn't reason with the fact that *my daddy* was touching and behaving this way with me. The same man that provided the seed that brought me into the world who was supposed to protect me had become my violator.

This was my wrestling buddy, my every other year bike-bringer, and also my once in a blue moon H&L Green downtown Dallas, Texas shopping buddy! What the hell is really going on here? On top of all of this, I couldn't even tell anyone! Who would believe me?

When I went to school I wondered whether everyone else's daddy was the same way. Were we all wearing secrets? I thought that there were others wearing secrets just like me. I would often try to answer myself, but the answers were vague, but the outwardly disguise was so well put together that I thought this was normal. You start to believe that this is normal, because it is happening to you and you begin to function as if you were a regular Joe or Jean. This could not be going on in my life right now. "Because I go to church" was my logic for why it should not be happening to me.

What would people think? What would my mother think? Will he kill me if I tell? Will he hurt my mother? All of the possible questions that could be asked by a child were bouncing like ping pong balls around in my head. Fear of rejection if I told, and even the fear of dying was constantly on my mind. I worked so hard at trying to forget what happened, that I almost forgot that he touched and kissed me in all the wrong ways. Again, I wanted to erase the thoughts of the nightmare and move forward as if nothing really happened.

Every part of who I was had been effected by what "the naked man" did to me that day. I did not know how to react to normal everyday situations, so I began to work hard on what I could keep normal in my life. I was naturally an achiever, so I ensured that my grades were not affected by my not knowing how to handle myself.   I was learning to develop a new normal behavior, so I thought... but my attitude with others was a trip around the world and back!

Working so hard to keep up with this *new normal*, I

didn't realize that I had become so insecure within myself. I became paranoid. I always thought somebody was talking about me, and I never really fit in with the "in-crowd" of other girls. That's when I began to seek love, affection and acceptance from boys. No, I didn't become sexually involved with boys at that age. I didn't know how to engage with boys my age in that manner. My first sexual encounters were with men – or should I say "adult boys." Men had set a sexual precedence, in my life and that precedence destroyed a natural development of liking boys in a sexual way which shouldn't have been normal to a girl my age.

In addition to becoming insecure about myself, I also developed a defense mechanism...fighting. I fought in school like it was a part-time job or a "side hustle." Beginning in the fourth grade I started getting expelled from school, but I still always managed to be on the honor roll. "Ms. Mouth Almighty" was my name and never did I let anyone push me around. Did I win all of my fights? Heck, no! Anger and rage was in my heart so I acted out by fighting. Fighting was my way of sheltering the secret inner-me that I was hoping no one could see.

I am the only child my mom has. I was a loner and I am still one until this very day. When you grow up without siblings and you are the oldest grandchild on your mom's side of the family, life can be jacked up. I felt as though I never had anyone to protect me. I remember in the fourth grade starting a fight with my boyfriend. He was only standing up as a fellow student to tell me to sit down and not to sharpen my pencil while the teacher was gone. He must have been out of his ever loving mind to tell *me* anything. I already had issues that no one understood because of the inner scars. I told him off like a half-pint sailor with a few cuss words to show that I did not take mess from anyone. "Ms. Mouth Almighty" had mouthed her way into a physical altercation. When I realized that fighting was inevitable, I didn't back down, not one bit! That was one physical fight that I had actually won! Looking back, I often wonder how such a high-achieving, smart girl seemed to always get in trouble. Then I gently remind myself that I was carrying a lot, and trouble was a silent outcry for help

The Good Ol' Days

It was not surprising at all that I was in a talented and gifted class. Someone noticed early on that I was above average. I believed they noticed in the second grade and I continued to show this giftedness until I reached high school. Thank God for some of our teachers back then. I had one that was truly like a mother. She was sharp-witted and quick with the stick, and I always seemed to be in trouble with her. I recalled a time when she whooped me because I didn't have my homework. For the love of God, I remembered doing the homework, but I had forgotten where I placed it. I remember sticking loose-leaf homework papers in my books until it was time to turn it in. When it was time to turn in the homework I looked and looked, but I couldn't seem to find it. I could feel it in my gut - I was headed for trouble. Even now, I can hear her saying, "Sista Zanderson, where is your homework?"

I was about to piss in my pants because I knew that the yardstick that was wrapped with masking tape was about to connect with my skin. She acted like "Zorro" when she whipped it out. I swear it had some hidden metal in-between the wood and the tape and I did not want to experience my punishment from her.

I tried to explain to her how extremely sick I was, but my teacher was not hearing it! When I told her that I was ill she laughed, whooped me, and then sent me to the office. Once the nurse saw me, she discovered that I really did have a high fever and it was to the point of going into a coma; at least that's what I heard my mom say. After 'The Great Beating of the Second Grade,' she came to apologize and informed me that they had located my work in my book. That became one of those whippings when they discovered that it was undeserved, so they excused it by counting it for something else you're going to get into later. Aside from all of that, she was a remarkable teacher and one that I will never forget."

"Judge, I wanted to reference this account so you could see that my life really did start out on the right track. I am sorry to get off focus and reflect on the good times I had as a child, but I really did not have too many of those. All of this is painful, but it must be told."

"Proceed, my dear," the Judge said.

I continued.

"Okay. As far as I can remember, after going to our first wrestling match I don't remember my dad trying to touch me again. Afterwards, I tried to continue on with my life as usual and pretend that I was normal.

I went on as if nothing had happened and prayed that I would not have to deal with this again. I tried to focus on the positive things that were occurring in my life.

I remember being a cheerleader for a Little League Football team, and I recall that my mother only came to one game out of the two years that I cheered. My grandmother despised the entire idea of my cheerleading at that time. She was old-school and thought that church, school, Saturday's washing and shopping was the meaning of life! Thank God for cousins and neighbors. I was not ashamed to beg for my aunts and uncles to find space for me to tag along with them during their family activities. I wanted to be included in family time. If I didn't ask, then no one would spend time with me. My mama was too busy living her life. My granny was too busy trying to make ends meet, and she did a great job of it. However, I didn't have a long list of people to choose from to do those child-like things with. I had to reach out to those who I knew were doing the fun things!

I had one aunt that had two little ones of her own, and sometimes she would take us skating or swimming. She was the fun aunt. She was the first person to introduce me to the arcade life, and the rest was history. I became a pro! (Thank you very much, auntie!) You could not tell me that after Midway Manufacturing's Ms. PAC-Man made its debut, that I wouldn't become the world's greatest player - especially on the ones that went super-fast when the ghost would launch an attack and eat you up in a blink of an eye! A little of Nintendo's Donkey Kong and Atari's Centipede was not outside my league either.

This aunt showed me how to be a kid. She would correct me when I got out of line, but gave me the love and attention that I needed. I was grateful for her. Since I was being raised around adults, my place was typically outdoors. I had the hoolah-hoop, lemon twist, jump ropes, jacks and my pink Huffy bike with the motor-cross seat. All of those things were good, but I longed for the time that I could have shared with my mom.

A Desire for a Normal Family

Little did I know back then, my mom had her own issues that she was dealing with. There were moments in her life that was not all that bad. I was so glad when she had married "husband number two." The feeling of family was great. I could remember finally having a sense of security and enjoying my own family. I was grateful for being the child that grandma took in, but I wanted to experience what my cousins had experienced; a mom and dad in the same household. Family is extremely important and creating memories with one another is something to cherish.

I once remembered my mom and my stepfather sneaking me in the only drive-in movie theater we had back then... "The Astro Drive-In". I was kind of confused because I had one parent trying to teach me martial arts by watching it - the other spooked the hell out of me with all those scary movies. Before I go any further with this, Your Honor, let me clarify that I am not trying to destroy my parents or anyone that crossed my path by opening up and finally coming forth with my story. For once I am allowed to tell my story. My testimony should have been heard in some judge's courtroom years ago, but I believe this platform serves best and will have the ability to reach many. As the Judge, you know there are not only two sides to a story, there are many sides when you have witnesses. But somewhere in all of those stories is the truth!"

I was glad when the judge spoke up,

"Go ahead and proceed," he said.

"One time I went to visit my paternal grandmother, and again I was faced with yet another act of someone not being able to keep their hands to themselves. I would love to go visit my paternal grandmother because she was going to make sure that the wrestling matches were a weekly event; and not to mention, she loved ice cream. She was good to me when I visited her and I would love the attention that she and my grandfather would give me. This woman (my grandmother) had a routine that kept everyone on task. The household knew what to expect - from Sunday's dinner to her Friday night visits to the Sportatorium. Then on Saturday, she would make sure that the half of gallon of Polar Bear's Hawaiian Delight Ice Cream was available as she waited for 'Saturday Night Wrestling' to come on television. As soon as 'Hee-Haw' would go off, wrestling would come on next, and wrestling to her was like another woman's soap opera.

I did not know any better but to think that my paternal grandparents were rich judging by the house that they lived in and the type of food that they ate. They seemed to be able to afford all of the things that I was not able to receive in my maternal grandmother's home. This was because the dynamics of the household were totally different. In fact, it was like comparing apples to oranges; a single mother and grandmother to a two-grandparent household. When I visited them we had the good, sweetened cereal, the big loop ones with all the fruity flavors, opposed to the cornflakes that you had to put a cup of sugar on. I don't want to come off as being ungrateful, but I need to explain why I thought my grandparents were rich.

My grandpa and grandma had two living areas, built-in dark wood bookshelves, and central air and heat. Central air and heat was like heaven because I come from a household where fans and window units were the central air and heat.

The first window unit I remember was a straw unit. I know for some of y'all it sounds ancient, but we had one. Wetting the straws was one of my responsibilities. I really hated when the summer consisted of those scorching hot Texas days because I was out there wetting straws for what seemed like every five minutes. Then some mean grown-up tried to punk me with, 'don't be so loud in the house or you're going outside.' If only a grown-up would recognize that the coolness of the window unit was because of my hard work. If only I could be appreciated for the hard work that I was forced to do.

You can clearly agree with me when I thought central air and heat was only granted to *the wealthy ones*.

Well, the next incident was at my grandma's house; the house of my dad's mom. We had come back from the wrestling match and she had me go sleep in the room next to theirs. Well, I thought it was odd because that night it seemed like everybody was gone. That room belonged to one of my uncles at the time, and he was not there. The only sound I heard was the dog barking in the backyard. As I was sleeping and getting into one of those deep sleeps which probably included that restroom dream that so many of us had and got beat nearly half to death for. You know the one, where you think that you just made it over the toilet and then you wind up in a bed full of pee? Waking up from that type of dream would have been much easier to handle than the reality of waking up to my dad on top of me, with his fingers in my vagina and him telling me not to scream or cry. He was so mean to me and I was afraid of him because of his angry demeanor, and how I would see him treat his wives and girlfriends. After he was done doing what he does, I remember him telling me to go wash myself up and that I better not tell anybody.

This particular night left yet another memory where a rotten seed was planted. That seed was so deeply rooted from within that the blood flowing through my veins seemed to have halted very quickly. This was a visit that I could not forget at granny's house and she had no idea what took place right under her roof. I lived in shame and guilt in a world thinking that no one cared about me anymore.

When I think about the grandmother that I lived with – man, she worked so hard to make ends meet for us. She was an upstanding missionary in the church, but what I saw in her and always heard from her was 'you know better than that.' That phrase has followed me like a shadow from the time I was a toddler up until now. Did I really know better than to withhold this type of information from my grandmother? Did I know what to do from a toddler and even as a young girl? Was I capable of handling this type of situation without informing an adult?

I couldn't tell my mother because she was busy living her life and doing her own thing, at least that's what I thought. I couldn't tell my grandmother or other family members. The idea of sharing this kind of information with strangers was frightening to me. So, who was a girl to tell? Who would hear me? I didn't know. Confusion started to creep in again and I just didn't realize how much power I had to expose this situation. I knew that what was happening to me was wrong, but I was also very ashamed and afraid about what could happen to me if I told. So here we go with the questions again that often went unanswered. Would he kill me? Would mama believe me? Did anyone *really* care enough to make a difference in the situation?

Fortunately, I was able to carry on as if nothing happened. I didn't really talk about what was going on in my life to anyone. Everyone was pretty much doing their own thing, and so was I. Whether they were raising kids, going to work, paying bills, or attending church and school this is how the average household functions, right? Now, I know someone in this darn family could have recognized that *something* was different about me. For instance, my breasts were huge for a girl my age. I was very curvaceous and smart-mouthed. My attitude was jacked up and fighting was only a word. These are certainly a few tell-tell signs of a child that is going through some type of emotional disturbance. I sought love in all the wrong places.

Do you know how it feels to be in an environment and everybody knows your name and yet they really do not know you? I could surely relate to this feeling. When I was growing up, as a child your voice was only recognized when orders were being given and the fact that you thought that your opinion was valued was a non- factor. When you are reared by old school hands and with old school expectations, it was your responsibility to live up to it, or try to anyways. I had a constant battle of trying to see which was going to win on a daily basis; the positive side of me that delves into maintaining good grades and trying to function as normal as possible, or the negative side that yielded to fighting and disruptive behavior.

In the midst of all of the turmoil that was occurring in my life, I was one of the young girls that was fortunate enough to start her period in elementary school. I had my fair share of making fun of the other girls that went before me, acting immature and laughing and carrying on as if my day wasn't going to come. Oh, but when it did, I will never forget it. The idea of wearing white pants was nothing but the enemy and yes, I had them on during this time of transitioning to womanhood. How lucky was I? My mind fails me on the type and color of my top, but my pants were white. I was looking cute that day until that afternoon in the nurse's office. Crying was an understatement. There I was, clueless and not knowing what to do. All the information in those *Life Cycle* books they had bought me left my mind at the time when I really needed it. It all just totally abandoned me. You know the routine. You go to the nurse and she gives you a pad, calls your mom then you go home. Your parents stop at the store to get some more pads and baby powder and some of that imitation cologne spray and you are good to go. Don't forget the aspirin for the cramps.

Still new to this process, I put it on wrong. It slipped and slid from my panties, and then Granny added her old-fashioned wit in the mix. She told me to line my underwear with a rag whenever I was in an emergency situation. Heck, with her remedy to help with "Ms. Flow" made me feel as though I was a flooding Wonder Woman! Yes, a little black superhero with white rags and pads that made me ready for liftoff. They did what was necessary at the time in the old days, and of course they did not have the luxuries as we do today, however; even the thought of the rag method was very ancient to me. This was something that I only heard about, not something that I was actually trying to re-live in my lifetime.

Still not grasping the fact that womanhood had set upon me, my character began to change. My play habits died and worrying started to get the best of me. I was not taught how to time this stuff. For the longest, this time of the month was referred to as 'my monthly' and that was cool with me. So my crazy self would mark my calendar as if it was going to come the same date every month. It did not occur to me that I did not receive the complete memo. The pregnancy lectures were coming like strong windstorms in the desert because *now* they considered me to be a young woman. Confusion still lurked. Remember, the furthest that a boy ever got with me was a kiss, so the full understanding of what womanhood was and what 'my monthly' meant was still very confusing.

Returning to the Present
The judge ordered a recess until the next day. He

stated,

> "Ms. Zanderson we will continue with your testimony on tomorrow and court is adjourned until ten o'clock tomorrow morning. You are dismissed."

I was kind of glad this was about to come to a close for that day. Sitting there and having to tell my story after all these years brought back some tears, pain and a slew of questions. Now, since I have the rest of the evening to myself, relaxation is a must. Since this was a Monday, not too much was going on but bible study later on tonight. Attending bible study on tonight was absolutely a must considering today's events. First on the list is to go home and get a nap in before the kids get out of school.

My mind had to rest before all of my daughter's teenage-girl news is released in the car. On the way home, I decided that some chicken from The Shack was a delightful choice for lunch. This chicken shack is the bomb. The chicken is cooked with straight lard and it is so good that even chickens go there to eat. Indulging in fried chicken and with side items that consisted of white bread (sloppy wet from pickle juice), French fries, hamburger-style dill pickles, and jalapeno peppers is the best lunch choice in the world. Please let me not forget to include the strawberry soda. You could not tell me that it was not the best bird around! I am glad that I decided to stop here for lunch before I went home.

I proceeded to eat my favorite chicken and watched a little trash television. By this I meant raunchy talk shows. You know the ones where so much DNA testing is going on, and the common phrase repeated is, "do you know who your baby daddy is?" I am so tired from jogging my memory of events at the courthouse, so caring about someone else's baby-daddy is the last thing on my mind.

I must have crawled up in my bed and went at it. Have you ever been so tired that an hour seemed like a day? Resting my body and mind was well deserved. My nap was interrupted because it was soon time to go pick up the children. The thought of wishing for siblings to share in some of my motherly duties were often than none; like picking up my children from school, came to my mind. One of my scriptures that I often quote is, "to whom much is given, much is required." My perspective of this particular scripture does not only reflect what we acquire in a material or financial sense, but also alludes to our responsibilities in life as well.

A single parent with two beautiful children, a mother who cannot drive, and no siblings, qualifies me for having a full plate of responsibilities. God has given me the shoulders to carry such tasks, and if you ask

Him, He will say, "she's doing quite well."

I usually like to allow each child to have their opportunity of being picked up first as the other wait for my services. My oldest daughter is the lucky one today. I try and rotate my routine, and to also show that I can be a fair chauffeur. Unfortunately, both of them get out of school at the same time, but they are three grades apart. One is in high school and the other in middle school, and luckily their campuses are ten minutes apart. I sarcastically congratulate the smart person or persons that thought of releasing both high school and middle school students at the same time. If I am fifteen minutes late, the oldest daughter gives me a certain look as if the silver taxi just ticked her off from arriving too late. We always greet each other and discuss the events of each other's day. Remember, being blessed with two teenaged daughters is sometimes a J.O.B. (Juggling over Boys).

While my oldest daughter and I were discussing the future of driving lessons, my youngest daughter began to interrupt with what happened to her at school during the day. This is typical of her; she enters the car, we greet each other with what happened at school, and then she is off to ask for money to buy something to eat. This child's metabolism is out the roof! The three of us jammed to the rap music, then gospel selections, and of course, I must hear my jazz or old school R&B. We would laugh and fuss about what happened to us throughout the day. This was our bonding time which occurs for a few hours each day after school. The ride home is our time to listen, interrupt, relate, and often release. I had to pretend that today was as normal as any other day. I could not let on that I was the star witness in the trial of my life! The only thing they knew was that I was tending to business every morning, and I had to be away from work for a while.

They asked, "What are we eating for dinner?" Since it was bible study night, we decided on the old American favorite of hotdogs, and today we added chili. What a blessing it was to have some good old chili to put on our hotdog. It was plenty of days that bun, meat, ketchup and mustard was the gourmet dish.

"Do you have homework? Do you have your clothes ready for the next day?" I ask these two questions every day, so without fail I would expect an answer. Without complaining they knew to give an answer even if I did not agree with it. You would think that new questions would arise in our household but I hold strong to being consistent.

They had their homework to occupy them for a little while before church service. That was good for me. I had to set aside special time to prepare for a spa bath tonight to unwind from the day's events and prepare for another day of testimony. While I was reflecting and preparing I begin to reflect upon my spiritual walk and I didn't want my progress to be negated by revisiting the life from my past. I needed lots of meditation and prayer tonight because of the trial.

I realize that I'm in a season of experiencing spiritual growth. I have grown in some areas, but I still have so much growth ahead. I am in a moment of my life where I do not want to return to the place to which I have just visited, and yet moving forward is also frightening. Whether that place is loneliness, addiction, or a place of not being satisfied with myself and others; whatever the case may be, I do not want to return. I begin to question God about why all of this happened to me. Why me, Lord? When you are raised from the old school hands, usually you hear people say one should never question God. Well, as much as I grew up hearing those words, it still puzzled me as to why we cannot ask why. Being the hard-headed individual that I am, I proceeded to ask God anyway. 'Why, God? Why me?' Although, I did not hear an answer instantly, I knew that I would eventually get one. I believe that somewhere down the road I will understand all of this.

My only request to God as I went into my prayer closet was for him to give me strength to make it through this week and to maintain my composure while on the witness stand. Knowing that time was getting close for church, these two young ones fell asleep as they often do when homework is involved. But somehow they managed to finish it.

"Y'all only have forty-five minutes to get ready for church," I yelled.

All I could do was envision that they were in their rooms rushing to get ready and probably putting the death wish out on me as most kids do to their parents when they don't want to do something. The soft sounds of murmuring and closet doors opening and closing were the only ringing that was coming through to my ears. Then it's,

"Have you seen my brush? I can't find my shoe. Have y'all seen my keys?"

We all take turns raising our voices trying to sort out the chaos that three females in a household have while rushing to get ready and leave the house.

As we were traveling to church, the topic of where we are going to sit once we arrived became the talk of the car. We all had our favorite spots to sit in church, and this is when playing the mommy card wins. Since I come from old school roots, my church mannerisms were not too far out of reach. I did not allow my children to go sit by their friends to "cut-up" while the teaching was going on. My children and I have been friends for a long time and what a better friend to sit by in church than me. Never was that a question or argument from them because they never had an option. I was always taught to "train up a child in the way you want them to go."

As we participated in praise and worship service, guess who followed me to church? It was the enemy. The enemy began to usher in the negative self-talk that reminded me of all the bad that occurred in my life. I tell you, the devil is mighty bold to follow a Christian to their home court - church. He does it all the time, and will continue to if you don't put him in his place. I began to rebuke him and say, "Go back to where you came from. You will not taunt me in my Father's house."

As the pastor was about to get into his message for the evening, all I could think about was the next day on the witness stand. It took a minute for me to get into the Word. To put a halt to the negativity that was swarming around in my mind, I recalled the scripture in Matthew that talks about each day bringing about its own anxiety. This scripture allowed me to get refocused on the Word and to concentrate on the now instead of what was going to happen on tomorrow. As our pastor was explaining how we are to forgive one another and those who have hurt us in the past, I thought of how timely a message we were receiving.

He used this example about a monkey being on your back as a representative of your troubles, and how you must get rid of them. It sounded ridiculous, but when I saw that stuffed monkey that grew into a big ape on his back, I really got the picture. The visuals that our pastor uses are so vivid, and yet simple enough that even a toddler could understand it. The lesson was very much needed and the timing could not have been any better for me. I had so many monkeys that *"George of the Jungle"* didn't have anything on me.

That night, longing to sleep in the sanctuary was a dream. Have you ever gone to church only to leave the building feeling that what was said was good, but very hard to apply in your personal life? I understood that forgiveness was essential to move forward, but applying it was difficult.

My thoughts are interrupted by one of my girls asking,

> "Mama, can we stop and get something to drink on the way home?"

Swearing is bad (so I've heard), but I swear that kids only go to church to find out what they are going to eat and drink afterwards. Their little souls are fed and that is enough. So we jump in the car and headed straight home.

It is approximately ten o'clock and the only thing I

could think of is sleep. It's like sleep and I had this special relationship as if we were best friends.

> *"Did you guys iron your school clothes for tomorrow?"*

It is amazing how selective hearing seemed like a core subject that must have been taught at school.

> "I know y'all hear me."

Knowing that tomorrow is only a few hours away, panic began to set in. The girls are ironing clothes and the youngest one knows how to get to me by lighting the candles. If they can soothe my nerves, then all of us can get along.

Even the scent of my favorite candles couldn't erase my anxiety about the coming day. There were so many questions that became assumptions in my mind, including what will take place on the witness stand. Stress was settling in before the ten o'clock news went off. I was nervous as all get out about the events planned for the next day. It was time to go to bed, say goodnight and shut the door to my room. Now, it was time for me and my Father to have some very special moments. The Heavenly Father, that is. Our time is very precious and the conversations are out of this world.

When I talk to God it is as if my best friend is listening to me. Sugar-coating my prayer with that dignified talk, such as, "Oh Lord of Host, the most Sovereign of them all, Father of infinity," tends to make my mind drift, and I would begin to think about everything but talking to God instead of staying on track. So instead, it is usually like this,

> "Look, Daddy your daughter is down here confused and just about to bless someone with a cussing out for cutting in front of me today, so help this attitude of mine. I need you Lord."

Now *that* is real.

We begin to talk. The conversation got good, and after a few minutes passed the session was over. I felt good about approaching the witness stand the next day because of the comfort that I received from my Father. Resting through the night was a challenge, but at least my mindset was in check.

Day Two:
"What Didn't Kill Me Made Me Stronger"

It wasn't too long before the alarm went off at 5:30am. It was Tuesday, and I could've slept for another half hour. Actually, all of us girls would've enjoyed sleeping in. That youngest one, would home-school if it were a choice. After all sleep, is also her best friend.

I woke up for the last time. It was now forty-five minutes later and the drill sergeant in me comes out boldly with, "Rise and shine ladies." I'm really a softy in the mornings and very concerned about how they rested the night before. The sergeant is ready to make sure all bunks are made and no time for horseplay. Sometimes you can tell when your children want to say things to you that will put them in a position of seeking instant medical attention. I have a distinct definition of discipline. I believe there is a fine line between regulator and aggravator. This particular morning, I was glad that we all got dressed in the privacy of our own rooms. The moment when you have to share a bathroom with two young ladies, your love begins to become conditional.

We quickly got dressed and jumped in the car to head

to school. After dropping them off at each of their schools, I headed back home to get ready for court. There was a moment of peace to really think things over while I was getting dressed. I thought that this day was going to be easier than the day before, but boy was I wrong.

While driving down the highway, my mind seemed to drift and focus on the weight of all that is going on. Before I knew it, warm tears began to stream down my face. I guess I hadn't realized just how sensitive and emotional this trial had made me become. I had waited for such a long time for someone to finally hear my side of the story, and finally listen to secrets that were screaming from within.

Driving in downtown Dallas, TX is stressful in the mornings. You come across streets that you thought yesterday were two-way only to find that you are on a one-way street. Construction sites are everywhere and my attempt to find a parking meter was impossible. I was nervous about resuming the testimony. The only thing on my mind was my family and how others would think of me. When things such as this are forgotten about and swept under the rug, others' viewpoint of you becomes a major concern. I never wanted to hurt anyone, but I knew that the truth had to be told and heard. As I got out of the car and proceeded to the courthouse I began to pray and ask the Lord for strength.

"God you know my motives and this is your will. Let it be done."

This was a different courtroom setting than ones that I was familiar with. Usually we have to wait for the bailiff to ask for all to rise as the judge enters the room. This time the judge was in position waiting for me. The audience consisted of family, friends and spectators. It was amazing to see that everyone was waiting for me. Some of them wanted to see what I was going to say, while others sat in with biased opinions already formed. They couldn't believe that after all this time the truth would be revealed.

"*Ms. Zanderson you may take the stand,*" the judge instructed. It was hard to believe that special treatment was given to me since I did not have any attorneys representing me. The judge asked me to proceed with the next encounter that I could remember.

"Well, I must go back to when all of us started our menstrual cycles in elementary school. That was the year help was on the way. There was this movie that came out where this young girl experienced some of the same things that I was going through. This is what started it all, me moving forward with telling someone what had happened to me. This movie was about this girl that was sexually abused by her dad. Tears began to come to my eyes when I saw it. The only thing that I could think was, 'That is me!' It was not too far along after watching the movie that I was moved to tell my teacher that something was bothering me. Really, Judge, I can't begin to tell you what prompted me to go to her instead of my mother or grandmother. I did not know what the outcome would be, but God must have known that I would be safe. The opportunity presented itself for me to tell my teacher what was going on with me. I believe this was the start of an action plan against the devil and his evil plan.

The school immediately called the welfare people as I had known them, also known as Child Protective Services (CPS). My mom came to the school and there we went. I had to go downtown the next day for questioning. That was the only time that I could remember that anyone ever interrogated me. It was a change from being told that I knew better than that – that is, to know better than to allow someone to molest me. After this, I often heard, "Why didn't you tell me?" This was coming from people that were around, but never really *around*. You get my drift. I was in a world filled with people who were not paying close attention to me, perhaps because life consumed them with many other responsibilities.

I remember my mother coming forth to make a report. We had to go to make a video of what was happening to me and to explain as best as I could about the horrible encounters of being molested. One thing that I can remember was the dolls that were used. There was a male doll with a flap and a female doll. I had to do a re-enactment of the whole situation, which was awkward for me. I had to use the hand motions, and I put one doll on top of the other, as if they were getting it on."

As I retold this part of the story, my mind quickly went to the judge to see his facial expression. Remember, I am finally coming out to tell what my daddy did to me and at the time I was not aware of all the legal issues that were involved. Then I drew a blank. I know this is on record somewhere and the videotape is still secretly filed away. The judge questioned,

"What happened after this?"

"Really, Judge, the only thing that comes to my remembrance is that life just went on as normal. Of course I don't know if my mother ever confronted my dad about the situation or what took place. I do remember that for a while I didn't see him. I had a sixth grade graduation that he and my grandmother attended, but after that, I can't say that I saw him much. We may have talked occasionally, but honestly, I don't remember much communication with him during that time.

My sixth grade year was very exciting and rewarding. I

hope you don't mind me reminiscing, but this was truly a year of triumph for me. Academically, and socially, I was able to participate in activities in school and be part of school related organizations that helped boost the esteem that often lay in the dark shadows. That was the time in my life when I began to realize that anything and everything is possible when I made up my mind to excel. I was the Student Council President. Also my best friend and I were competing in a Spelling Bee competition. She eventually won. I was now experiencing positive and healthy activities in my life. That year trophies and certificates were plentiful. Despite all of the hurt and disappointment I was dealing with at home, my "rebound spirit" was in full effect during this part of my childhood.

Although I was doing well in school, I couldn't help but face all of the pain I was feeling when I would go back home. My accomplishments didn't erase the pain, shame and self-blame that I was harboring. My experiences had taught me that sex was love, and that was my truth for many years. That one little whisper from my father, 'When you want to feel good you know where to come,' had really messed me up."

I paused to think about those words, and before I knew it, I stormed off and left the witness stand in tears. I ended up in the restroom. The weight of my emotions had gotten the best of me, yet I couldn't help but think about what everyone was thinking about me. I knew that I needed to return to the witness stand and get past this painful memory. I was glad that the judge had granted an hour recess because my meltdown lasted almost that long.

After stepping away from the witness stand and going to an hour-long recess, I was able to regain my composure. I have given a lot of testimony already, but I still had a lot to go. Remember, all of the events I testified about up until now were from my toddler years through grade school. I still have to go back and explain my life as a young teen and what I had to face as an adolescent.

I went back to the witness stand and continued to tell of how I was looking forward to going to middle school and I thought I was a little grown up. Actually being *a little grown* is an understatement because being involved in grown-up situations had replaced childhood and school-aged memories.

"Judge, I really got tired of growing up with titles like 'Hot Mama' or 'Fassy'. Now those names didn't come from my family but young girls and older ones in the community who thought they knew me. My hair was short at the time, my self-esteem was extremely low, and my figure was enough to capture a man, but too thick for a young man my own age to even look twice or want to date me. People must realize that there is a point in a girl's life that every move she makes and every mood that is encountered is critical to her well-being. Anything that you say to us during the adolescent phase of our life is always viewed as truth. My wardrobe was not the best because that was my semi-sanctified days of being in the Holiness church. My fashion statement was cool for church, but for school, definitely not. My grades were beginning to slip because of all of the emotional and mental roller coaster rides I had been on.

The next predator was my gym coach. He later became my lover. Never did I go to my seventh period in the seventh grade. Well, it seemed that way because he would always come and get me out of class. Now I must tell you parents once again, watch your children. Know your children! For those of you who do not have kids of your own, but have a hand in raising other's kids, please pay close attention to the hidden signs of abuse. My coach was a predator, too.

Yes, ladies he was fine and cute and all of us loved him. When we went down the halls he would stop traffic like a freight train. His color was caramel. He was about 6'3" and his muscles were eye catching. The northern accent that he possessed captured the majority of the young girls. Being that we were straight from the hood, anything sounded good to those of us that were not exposed too much.

Now, you know he should have been under the

jailhouse, too. I never told anyone because they were becoming my boyfriends; the predators, that is. When I didn't have young boys giving me any play and the only play was coming from the big dogs, then that is what I allowed myself to put up with. No one in the family knew about these...I call them 'encounters'. God and any of the nosey young men in the locker rooms could have witnessed these encounters. First, it was just a few encounters with "Coach", but he continued to prey upon my low self-esteem and vulnerability that the encounters grew large in number. It began to happen so frequently, that I couldn't keep up with the number of times that he actually came to get me out of my class. Now, this was not "the life" for a thirteen-year-old girl. This certainly wasn't the life I had hoped for at my age.

My life at age thirteen was more experienced than some women that was twice or maybe even triple my age. Because of my experiences as a toddler, I often thought that "this" was normal, and that the average girl was going through all of this unwanted drama and abuse. Although my uncle didn't bother me during my 7th grade year, he had his fair share of sneaking in my room and taking advantage of me in every way possible by touching me inappropriately. If I could place a marker on the age of my uncle's inappropriateness, I will guess from about ten years old is when he began to sneak in his feels. However, when we moved out of the house into the apartments, all hell broke loose.

My 8th grade year was hellacious. My life was not turning for the better, but for the worse. I thought that the move would have been that of protection especially since I did not have my coach as a lover anymore. When we moved and I lost whatever little friends that I had gained. Our new location was in a different part of Oak Cliff, and no one was coming that far to visit me from my old neighborhood. The new school was so uppity and the girls were ghetto fabulous. I can remember going across this bridge every day and arriving at school only to be frustrated to see that people my age being dropped off in cars that I only dreamed of someday owning. Coming from the family where new cars didn't consist of the Porsches, BMWs and Mercedes I was now seeing, I marveled at the vehicles that my classmates' families owned.

I thought that attending this new school would be a great change in my life. It was. The fighting ceased and we moved away from "The Coach", and that was good for me. I started to go to the sock-hops and school dances to feel a sense of normalcy in my life. A few friends came my way for a change, but I always felt like the lonesome dove mixed with the ugly duckling. My sexual urges ceased only momentarily during this new season in my life. Some of the boys began to notice me but only because of the aggressive personality that was instilled in me. Remember, I thought that sex was love. That was the only definition of love from a man that I could relate to.

I finally got attention from a decent young man who later became my boyfriend. This guy had to be about fourteen years old, so I thought since we both were in the eighth grade. I think that part of my attraction to him was that I thought he was part of the "misfit club". He was tall and goofy and pretty much a loner at school, but I later discovered that he had admirers! Misfit my behind! He may have started off as a misfit until a young seventh grade girl had her eye on him; and then suddenly he became "popular". We went together for a few months. After finally landing a real boyfriend in my life I realized that I had shamefully allowed grown men to touch me inappropriately and be with me in the worse way, so that I never wanted to be sexually active with young men my own age."

Dealing with Regurgitated Emotions
I stopped for a minute.

> "Judge, can we please stop for today my flashbacks are really getting me sick at the stomach?"

> *"Yes. Court is adjourned and we will begin at 9:45 a.m. tomorrow morning."*

"Thank you for your understanding."

As I left the witness stand and headed to the elevator, tears begin to fall once again. My emotional state was not one of pity, but of confusion. A barrage of thoughts and questions hit me all at once. 'Why had this happened to me? What sort of person was I to allow it to continue? Why didn't I tell someone sooner than I did? I must be mentally sick to have allowed men in my family to sleep with me. What was my problem? You are no good! You will never amount to anything! You're a slut! You're a whore! No one wants you and you'll never be with anyone that loves you! No one loves you! How can you live with yourself?' These types of statements and questions lived with me for years and going to my car, I recalled all this negativity. This day was mentally stressful, more than I had truly prepared for.

Being on the witness stand for two days in a row is mentally and emotionally draining. I had to first be brave enough to want to share this part of my life with the public. Traveling down this road to recovery has not been easy for me. Today is one of those days that I had to rely on the local jazz radio station to help get me through. Not only do I have to regroup and focus on my motherly duties that awaited me, I had to also try to forget all that was going on so that I would not be emotionally distraught once I met up with the girls. My thoughts were scattered. I was trying to forget about today's events by contemplating what to eat for dinner. This was one of those days that I really needed my children to give me a quick moment of alone time.

> *'Thank you for my children, Lord. Thank you for allowing me to depend on them for emotional support right now. I know you are always with me Father, but today I need a little laughter in my life. The few days were very eventful and I know that my children will do something to put a smile on my face.'*

These words were uttered quickly from my mouth without any type of rehearsal. As I finished talking to the Lord, I waited and heard a calm voice respond,

> *"It is going to be alright. They will understand you."*

"Who will understand me?" I questioned.

> *"Your children and your future husband will understand you."*

After hearing such a peaceful and assuring response, I immediately slipped into a moment of doubt.

"My future husband? Lord, where is this man? Lord, you know that I have been waiting a long time."

I felt as though there wasn't a man on this earth that would want me or accept me with this mess of a life that I had endured. Encouraging words once again whispered in my ear,

> *"At the opportune time you will have the one that was molded especially for you."*

I began to think to myself that my first marriage was not all that bad, so to experience someone just a little bit better would be nice. All of this conversation with the Lord, and all of these thoughts were going through my mind on the way home.

My emotions were very high and everything else were extra sensitive on this day. For the first time I thought of how much more special my life would have been if the vicious acts of molestation had not taken place. I traveled back and forth like that in my mind all the time while most of the family swept topics like this under the rug and at times, some of them made me feel as though I was beneath some of them.

I appreciated my children for being patient with me on this day, especially my oldest daughter. I believe that sometimes we have that mother-daughter twin syndrome. She knows me so well. She stepped up and asked to cook this evening's meal and demonstrated her ability to take care of mama and little sister. My children are not rookies to chores. When she talks about leaving for college, I begin to feel like one of my best friends are leaving me, but I know that time will be here when she will have to spread her wings and leave the nest.

Tonight is definitely a prayer closet night. This week has been tough for me so stealing a few moments to just go and pray and talk to God was well needed. I was not in a happy-go-lucky state of mind and neither was I in a mood that was impossible to deal with. I just needed some 'me' time. The worst thing that I could succumb to is all of the negative and strange thoughts that I had all throughout this trying day. I had to take time out to pray and usher in a positive and joyous spirit. I learned that it is very necessary to take a dump. I'm not talking about a bowel movement type of dump. It's necessary to dump out all the trash and negativity that comes your way and replenish it with good thoughts, good vibes, and good self-talk.

I have been taught that satan is the master of deception and confusion. His game plan is to make you feel as though you are crazy and cause you to belittle yourself. He knows that if he can get you to believe that nothing is possible and that no one cares about you, then it is over. That is a big fat lie! Since I was getting biblical teaching on how to recognize his tactics, it was becoming a little bit easier for me to recognize how this wicked spirit was coming at me. Not to say that I did not still fall into his traps, but now I have the ability to paralyze him and his wicked acts. I really thank God for the Word and teaching that is given to us in our church. It seems like what we are being taught is always very timely.

> '*Now Lord, you know your servant. Help me to deal with the past and the past hurts. Lord, you know that it's challenging for me to open up and discuss the abuse that occurred in my life. Although I have been waiting for a long time to get it all out Lord, you know how the public, my family and friends can criticize me before the verdict is even rendered. So Lord, look down on your daughter right now. Come in and give me peace of mind in knowing that it is all done. Lord, please remove discouragement, depression, anger, resentment from my heart and from my mind. Do you hear me God? Are you there? Your Word says that, you'll never leave me or forsake me, and now I am depending on you and your Word. Thank you for listening to me tonight. I love you Father.*'

Now, the last thing that I remembered was the infomercials asking people to buy some program to learn how to buy stock online. When the red lights began to flash on the alarm clock, I immediately thought it was time to get up for work.

I must keep reminding you that a sister that is single with kids and drama every day, well every other day, is not working with a full deck all the time. It was too early in the morning to even see straight, let alone be interested in some stocks with any company. I fell asleep with the Lord on my mind and only remembering a little of the conversation that we had and then I felt compelled to check the channels. I also was awakened to my favorite gospel song being sung by one of my favorite Gospel artists on television. I sat up in bed and proceeded to sing along. After bedroom church was over at about 4 a.m., immediately that little voice came to remind me of all the upcoming events. I kept hearing that negative voice that keeps reminding me of all the negative things in my life. You know, that scraggly voice that makes you paranoid, depressed and upset with the world. The voice that tells you that you will never amount to anything and nobody wants you. Can anyone relate to what I was experiencing? Once a person can identify and determine the voice of good and of evil then life can be a little less complicated. I just had to tell him (the devil) to hit the road and back to the pits of Hell you go! I didn't use my 4 a.m. bedroom voice. No. I used my James Earl Jones voice. You know, the one with strength, clarity and authority. Listen. Now, I may be short in stature, but that doesn't mean that I can't get my point across when I have to.

Day Three:
"Am I Mentally Corrupt?"

The next voice I heard were kids telling me that we had over slept this morning. That was bad for them but as for me everything was on task. This was going into my third day of testimony and as the week was coming to a close I knew that more information had to be revealed. Each day was getting tougher to be on the witness stand and somehow I managed to stay strong.

As I proceeded to drive to court this morning, I decided to listen to my favorite morning show on the radio and they were giving hood (ghetto) advice as usual. It consisted of three males and one female hosting the show. They were just too funny. I mean they were really hilarious, if you asked me. Listening to them cut up made me reminisce over events in my life that were happy. I needed to engage in a little laughter before taking the witness stand again, and this morning show was the cure.

I began to talk to myself in the car. 'Do you realize how much you have gone through, girl?' To carry on a conversation with myself was not the problem; it is when I begin to answer myself that a problem occurred. There are just some things that you just do not do and society has taught us not to answer ourselves. The drive going into downtown was a breeze. Traffic was not an issue and everything seemed to be tolerable. The drive time was not long enough, because I would have loved to stall. As much as I wanted to get this off my chest and finally release what has been bottled up for years, I also felt embarrassed to tell the whole truth and nothing but truth. In this scenario the truth *really hurts.*

The courtroom was filled with less than a hundred folks. That was still too many in my eyesight. A continent full of people is what it seemed like to me. There we were again. The people began to stare at me and some of the looks would have killed me spot on. If a look could truly kill, then I would have been assassinated once I entered the courtroom. Others that really did not know me but knew of me were amazed at my story, and from facial expressions many were in awe.

Some people started to gossip right in front of me. Some turned and whispered to their elbow partner, others made side-ways glances at each other, and a few even nudged the person next to them. You know I had to reach back and remember one of my pastor's lessons. Of course he teaches us all the time, but some information you hold onto more so than others. I could hear him saying, "there are two sides to every coin, and then there is the truth." "Always know *the why* behind it." Meaning, you cannot form an opinion based on one person's viewpoint of a situation.

My story is my perspective. My perspective houses my experience. My experience houses my truth. My story is my truth according to the things that I experienced and with whom I had experienced these things with. I am inclined to believe that you will never get the predator to come forth and admit to his or her wrongs. That will be the day. That will be a day of courage both on the victim and predator's part. It takes a strong person to admit that they are in the wrong and if any type of punishment is due, most will shy away and not accept what is coming to them.

Before I could continue from yesterday's events, I experienced a heckler in the crowd. I refer to her as a heckler because of the way she was responding. One of the women in the crowd began to respond in a negative manner and was acting rude and daring. She made this indirect outburst, which was directed at me. She wanted to know what possessed me to tell such a thing. She said, "Years have gone by and you just decided to tell this stuff?" This is not *stuff* I thought to myself. She did not realize that I overheard that absurd comment, but I did. I just kept my response to myself. The older I get, the more I have learned how not to respond to everything that is said to me. Actually she was not talking to me, but she was talking *at* me and that did not deserve my attention. It was difficult trying to ignore the comments that were flying over the room, and refrain from responding to the faces that did not give me much hope while sitting on this stand. We picked up at the part where I had this boyfriend and how before him I did not like boys my age.

"You know judge this is where I remember Devon being in my life momentarily. He met me at the eighth grade prom. You heard me say *met*, for he did not take me to the prom. Devon was a nice boy and attended church during the week and on Sundays. Their family attended church just as often as we did. He was not so nice after my grandmother thought she caught us "doing it." Back then we said doin' it and you know what it was...sex!

Well, here was the scene. It was one afternoon we all were up in Devon's cousin's house. We only kissed and boned (which is necking and heavy petting) and that was it. He never went all the way with me because first of all he really was a decent guy. I knew Devon's aunt well enough to know that she was not going to tolerate any hanky-panky mess in her house. On this particular afternoon, my grandmother decided that she would get out and hunt for me in the apartments and she found me indeed. I was good at turning purple because my face was too black to turn red. None other than my grandma stood right smack dead in the front door. The only thing I could see was her face looking with disgust and feeling her rough sandpaper hands going across my face.

She fussed at me so much, that sometimes I preferred a physical beating rather than those harsh words. She rarely would use profanity, and I probably could count on one hand the few times that I heard her slip with a cuss word. She would fuss royally and would continue on and say, "You know better than that." She had a way with making words stick to you hotter than grits on the fourth of July. While walking back to our apartment, my mind was racing and I was trying to convince her that "doin' it" with Devon never happened. She was not hearing it. She saw what she did not see and anything that I was thinking was held against me. Really, it did not go down. Only I know what happened to me that day and sex was not it.

Within that same summer weird things started happening to my body. I will never forget when we went over my cousins' house after church everyone went outside, but not me. I was in the house feeling feverish with my head just spinning. Growing up I really did not get sick that much, only a common cold or a fever. This was truly different and draining. My body began to feel very sluggish. I went on ignoring it for a few days and then it seemed like a drastic change came about immediately. Any foreign smell that came my way made me feel horrible. It was crazy. The aroma from food cooking, perfumes, colognes, stinky breath...you name it, my nose became very sensitive. My body revolted and I could not handle it. Well, this time if you had not guessed it by now you should have. I was pregnant, and, no, it was not Devon's baby.

My uncle had me for about a year. This particular uncle was very sneaky and would scare the hell out of me. He would crawl through windows to get to me. This man would be on the prowl trying to get at me when I was asleep. His sick shenanigans began back when we were in the house. I developed a phobia of not being able to sleep without some type of blanket on me. And this is all because of the way he would sneak into my room. This has stayed with me for life. It could be one hundred degrees outside, but I have to use a sheet or blanket to cover me while I am sleeping and I have been this way for years. Anyway he went too far that last time. My uncle was one of the perpetrators that would try to get at me every chance that he would get. I was running around the house sick as a dog. Throwing up all the time and still naïve as to what I was going to do.

I told him about my suspicion of being pregnant before my grandmother found out. He spent weeks trying to get money for me to get an abortion, but that did not come through. It was his idea that I drink nasty vinegar to end the pregnancy, and he would supervise while I drank the stuff. I had never heard of that until that time. I recalled being scared out of my mind. I did not know what to do. I felt that a train could have run over me and maybe that would have been better. He was so sneaky and yet very stupid at the same time.

Neither of us had a pot to piss in or a window to throw it out of. He was the eldest in this situation and acted like an idiot about all of it. Now let's dissect this situation. This was my uncle who planted his seed in my young womb, not some young man off of the streets. If this were not some tripped up soap opera scene, or better yet an episode of trash TV; I do not know what was. Reality is now in effect. This was happening and the only one standing accused is me. When I told my grandmother, she asked, "Why didn't you tell me?" Followed by what was her trademark words, "You know better than that." That is what she said to me after I told her that the baby belonged to her son.

She called me fast and a liar. It seems as if lying was my middle name to hear them tell it. Now, just one thing I would like to share with anybody that has been violated. **You _know_ who touched you and who did not!** Even a person that is blind can recognize a scent. My advice to any overcomer of sexual abuse is to know and believe that it is not your fault, and especially if you were a child. My world seemed as though it had come to an end once again. Y'all have to remember I was just entering into my teen years when all of this was occurring.

During this time, I was afraid; and that is an understatement. I was alone and terrified of the outcome. I must say that my thought process was one of a rebound spirit. I truly believe that God made me with the ability to forgive but I would rarely exercise my right to do so. When you have to live, eat, ride, depend and just be around those who have violated you the majority of your life, you learn to forgive. Notice that I did not say that I had forgotten the painful situations that I have experienced. The abuse was so painful that you just do not think you are going to ever make it or really fit into society. However, at that time in my life fitting into society was the least of my worries since I already felt like a misfit.

The main obstacle was this child and knowing that being a mother was the last thing I wanted or needed. Some girls wanted children or that one person to love them. On the other hand, I wanted love, but really I desired life! Can I just be a child, or now at this time what we call a *child teen*? I just wanted to be a regular kid without someone always trying to get at me. Really, my desire was to get away from it all and just be me. As time went on my morning sickness became unbearable. I could not eat, drink or smell. It was just terrible. Somehow my grandmother was able to get the money for me to have an abortion.

The day arrived when my grandmother took me to the abortion clinic. I was afraid, but in my heart I knew this was something that had to be done. I could not start high school with a child and the knowledge that the baby's daddy was my flesh and blood. Sitting in this room with these women and young ladies was very uncomfortable. It was cold in there. The room temperature was not just cold but you could also feel the coldness from the people. A few protesters were outside with their signs fighting against abortions.

Am I *for* life or *against* it?

My head was just spinning with questions such as, 'am I for life or against it?' I am a thinker by nature, but this was just a little bit too much for me to process. Being grown before my time was never my intentions, it just happened. It is a shame that I learned how to kill before I learned how to love. Looking for love in all the wrong places was not just a song, it was reality. It was my reality. I did not know how to love and at this time the title of 'murderer' was presenting itself strongly in my presence. I knew this place wasn't for me, or anyone else that was there seeking services.

This was the beginning of history. Mind you, beat downs were always in effect when it came to me taking medication. Trying to swallow a baby aspirin was a challenge for me growing up. My mother would go through drastic measures to get me to swallow a baby aspirin by dissolving the tablet in a teaspoon filled with water. That was pure torture. Have you ever had to break a solid down to a powder then all the substance in between taste like death was lingering at your door?

So here I am facing blood being drawn, IV's and a procedure that was very life-altering and intrusive. It seemed as if I was the only young girl there that was my age. My body and mind was not ready for all that I had to encounter. My passive attitude and knowing that there is a God helped me through this rough time. I will have to admit that some of us are forced to be strong. When winds blow your way and try to get the best of you either you sway with the wind or you just get knocked down. Swaying with the wind was my only option.

This procedure was scary. This surgery was considered an outpatient procedure that typically took a couple of hours. By the afternoon patients were released to go home if they didn't get sick from the anesthesia. I never had to get on the table and have someone stick a speculum inside me. That thing hurt! The speculum could do a world of damage if it's in the wrong hands. The law should require that doctors receive a certification as speculum specialist were my thoughts.

The last thing I could remember after the speculum was some nurse telling me to count from ten backwards. I do not remember making it to number one. The nurses and doctor told me that I would not feel a thing. They did not tell me the truth about what to expect, because I felt and heard the procedure.

My prayer was for God to forgive me. Even though all the abuse leading up to now was to rest on my teenage shoulder, I believed that God would somehow forgive me. However, I could not concentrate on the words from the prayer but my mind went to songs, Gospel songs. Songs tend to take on a different meaning when you have gone through something. Some of the lyrics to old hymns are enough to comfort you in your time of need. Those words are deep in your soul and you can just reach deep down and start to call out for help.

Now back to the table of pain. This was a time that I needed to rely on a Word and being that young, I really did not know too many scriptures or examples that could have related to my experience. I know you hear me, God. I need you!

'Why me? Why do I have to go through this Lord? How could I let this happen to me? This is my fault. I knew better than this. All of this could have been prevented.' Yes, it could have been prevented, but when you are touched as a baby and throughout your childhood sex become this drug that leads to a horrible addiction. Sex then becomes a bad habit that you really do not have any control over. You are eventually sucked into this trap that you did not ask to be a participant of. Even though you have others that added to your misery, you still hold all of the pain.

Everything seems to be moving so fast at this point of my life, judge. Getting a hold of my life was really a cliché. How can that be possible? Now, your honor, this is when I told you I believe that after this major event I started suffering from a memory loss. I never had this medically proven, but I can remember some things quite well. Then there are occurrences from about age fifteen through sixteen that just do not serve my memory.   This abortion was a catastrophic event in my life. It was one of those things that you did not speak about, but had to bounce back from and continue as if it never happened.

My recovery time was not six weeks - neither was it six years; how about a lifetime. This was difficult. The pieces of the puzzle were too difficult to try and put together. This abortion was just like going the full nine months, even though the pregnancy was terminated. I still had to live with months of pain and misery. No one ever told me anything about sex. You know the rules and regulations. Every game has rules and regulations. You can attribute that to any game including sports, board games, and also this one glorious game called life. Do I consider my life to be a game? Not really, but during this time of my life it appeared to be the game and I was left trying to win. I was just a pawn trying to find my way to the other side of the chessboard all while being misguided. I knew that not every person in my world intended to harm me, but the force of evil that controlled them put a good hurting on me.

Judge, I remember that it was not soon after the abortion that my stay with my grandmother was interrupted. My going to church came to a halt. I had a barrage of questions, such as, 'What am I going to do? Where am I going to stay? Who can take care of me like she can? Why am I the misfit child? Why I don't live with my mother and father like other children? Why can't I be like my cousins? They have their parents, one of them if not both. Lord, why did you bring me into this world for this?'

One thing that puzzles me until this very day is the question of who called the police. Since they thought I was such a liar and being 'Ms. Fassy,' I did not expect anyone to call the police. However, one evening the police came to our apartment. If my memory serves me correctly, my uncle was pulled to the side while they talked to him. The next thing that was said was I could not live there anymore. They started asking some questions, such as, 'Where are her parents?' My grandmother told them exactly how she raised me all of my life and both parents were still living. My mother had moved out of the city and I didn't know how to contact her. We searched and searched for her so that

I could have a place to live, but to no avail.

Resentment forever lingered in my mind. Sure I was taught in church from a child on up until now that you should not commit suicide, but suicidal thoughts were strong. I was taught that you did not have the right to take your life because you didn't give yourself life. What I was taught became a thing of the past at that moment, because I wanted to feel comfort and peace and ending it all was the solution that I came up with. Who would be willing to live after having an abortion and on top of that being removed from the only home they know of? Tears began to run continuously down my face.

> *"That will be enough for today. All arise! This court is adjourned until tomorrow morning at 9:30 am."*

Those words were welcoming to my ears. As the week progressed, I began to get where I couldn't take it anymore. My heart was heavy because of all the memories.

Can You Hear Me Now?

My time has finally arrived to tell this story, and yet I feel bad about doing so. It certainly hasn't been an easy task but it must be completed. To find an escape, I run to listening to music and writing lyrics and poetry. I find this as a way of release and somewhat of a therapy session. I felt the need to escape and listen to some music to revitalize my spirits after spending a long, hard day on the witness stand. On the way home from court I allowed this DJ to help me get in a more relaxed mood.

Spending a whole day talking about this kind of drama in one's life can drain you and also make you bitter. You really think that you're over it, and just when you have to confront it again, you see that you are not completely over the situation. I am healed! Was I lying to myself? I was healed from some of it but not completely from all of it. Isn't it amazing how you can slang snot, cry all day long, throw a pity party and still nobody shows up but you. When having a pity party, please don't forget to play your favorite song. One of my favorite songs that helped me to get through it all is *"Safe in His Arms."* Sometimes when you're listening to the rhythm and blues, your roots never fail to pop up- Gospel that is. More than enough, this was a trying week, and no matter how difficult each day was, I knew that I was Safe in the Lord's arms.

While driving in the car I begin to allow my mind to wonder in many directions. I begin to think that sometimes we live in a world of fantasy and of the unknown. We like to pretend that certain things never took place. Often we try to forget, but it seems to always be something to serve as a reminder. People, places, songs, books and thoughts many times assist us in returning to that place of bliss or that forest of burden. Our shield that we once put up as a defense mechanism is immediately torn down. Usually there is a moment when we experience a total melt-down because of the triggers that unknowingly assisted us to the place of no return, a temporary moment of depression. We prepare ourselves for what is common but the uncommon gives us a mighty blow.

In my case, the common was quite commonly uncommon because I have to see my predators quite often and speak to them as if nothing happened. I had to live with them. Eat with them. Laugh and talk with them and carry on as if we were good friends. The flip side of this is the uncommon. The uncommon and the uncomfortable were trying to engage in mature conversations about sex and virginity when you do not feel that you have a valuable contribution because you feel as though you cannot relate. I was still trying to comprehend that dating is not sexing.

As my mind began to travel down these different roads called "thoughts," I felt as though my shield failed me and there I was left unprotected. 'Loser! You good for nothing woman! You will never turn out to be anything! Look where you came from! You are too fat, and don't nobody want you! You are stupid for letting this happen to you.'

I found myself listening to all of that negativity and

then screaming out loud to make it go away. Stop it! Stop it! I was trying to drown out those insults. There seemed to be a constant battleground between my two ears. There is so much that is processed and yet the majority of it shouldn't have been retained. I am not the only one I know with this war going on in my head. I know that there are a many of us that have lived with the aftermath of sexual abuse.

Although this internal war was going on from within, I still felt a sense of being blessed to have children to go home to. I picked up my oldest daughter first. It was a chore to remember how to alternate between my two daughters when I was often trying to operate in fairness. You would think that she had to punch the clock. She does not like being late and yet she has a mom that is late to *everything*. I just might be late to my own funeral but I know that if the Lord leaves her in charge I won't be. She gives me a look like my grandmother when I am late picking her up. She is respectful but that look says a thousand words. She began to rattle off and I heard her, but then again I did not. After picking up my youngest daughter we went for the question of the day. What are we eating for dinner?

Sometimes I felt as though I was enslaved to these kids. They would send me off to work for eight hours and then expect me to feed them after work every day. What is a parent to do? 'I am not going to feed you ever again,' I said. Mentally I thought this but, I dare not say this to my children. Do you think that we as parents could ever dump these kids off and run away like some of them do us? I have often thought of giving up on them, but just could not do it. When I look into the eyes of my youngest daughter and feel the motherly presence from my oldest daughter, I only see the love that I always was seeking through and from them. The two of them was the best loan God could have ever given me. They fit right into my life.

This is certainly a pizza night for me because I did not feel like cooking. I was all for the local pizza buffet. With a buffet that offered pizza, pasta, and desert for $3.99 per person I could not go wrong, and the price was certainly within my budget.

Now my kids are being extra nice to me because they knew that the weekend was growing closer and they wanted to do something fun with their friends. I paid very close attention to the tactics that they were using to get on my good side. Luckily for them, I was concentrating on the moment that I had to relax and release all of the toxins that resurfaced this week. "You can't play the player" is one of my favorite clichés. This was a motto that I would live by so they would realize that I was aware of the game. I have come to realize that these children will play you like a mariachi band playing at a Cinco de Mayo event if you let them.

I immediately envisioned the candles aflame and a bubble bath filled with scents of Secret Crush from Victoria's Secret. After a long day of thinking and having to go back so far in my life and not being held to every exact word, was very stressful. I just wanted to relax and let my mind rest from all of the painful events of the past.

All I could think about was my private sanctuary and some of my favorite spa ensembles.   Since the increased popularity of bath gels, body sprays, lotions and potions, the female species has become very spoiled to pampering one's self. I figure, why not pamper myself with things that I like?

Just when I thought that I was going to enjoy my peaceful and relaxed night I get a phone call. It was a call from my distant love. I guess he was feeling ignored because I was not programmed to answer his call as he thought I should have.

"Hello," I answered.

"You just lied. I thought you were going to call me back last night. You are just like all the rest of them. Your cell phone just rang and rang. I am not crazy and you must have another man."

I was thinking to myself, 'You are crazy, and no I did not have another man present. Since you believe that, you can forget about me and this relationship.' The next thing that I heard was the sound of dead air. He hung up.

Being that I became a pro in dealing with difficult situations such as men tripping like that, I had this under control. Did he get a reaction out of me? No, he did not because I just learned how to forgive after attending a week of focused bible study at church. The best way to get some respect and closure from the enemy is to not speak. Defending yourself when you do not have anything to defend is crazy so sometimes you just have to let it go. I recognized the enemy with his crazy tactics. My mind was on having a relaxed evening, and that slight interruption attempt did not succeed.

Just when I thought my toe would hit the water for that bath, I found out that my cable was turned off. 'In the evening? They usually come early in the morning to disconnect the cable,' I said to myself.

Living this born again life is hard. My neighbor upstairs could go and hook it back up. That was only a thought. My neighbor was the "Hook-Up Queen". When her lights get cut off she would take her tools and turn them back on. I will never forget one day when we were coming home, "You did it mama," yelled a voice from the second floor window. That was her son alerting her that the cable was back on. Now you know cable is a service that we all try to get the hook-up on. However, on this evening my conscience would not allow me ask her to help us out. Remember this night is supposed to be one of relaxation. I've been told off, had my cable turned off and have been unsuccessful in taking my bubble bath.

My first thought is 'What's next?' The next thing was my bath, and yes, it was very soothing. I have been through a week of hell and this night has not made it any better. You know your elders can teach you a lot. The one thing I have been taught was never to say what is next. Even though I think that is superstitious, I believed it. A week would not be successful without a little baby daddy drama in my life. Mind you I was blessed with two of them. Both of them are sane but act insane at different times. I have never experienced them both acting up at the same time, thank God. I must admit often my attitude will contribute to the arguments. Okay, my attitude may contribute to more than half of the arguments, but we survived them all. It takes The Word and everything that is within me sometimes not to reach back and verbalize the profanity that comes to mind when I have to deal with my child's father. I have to be real about the situation.

This one we will call Mr. Suave. He was and still is a

lady's man. For years my nose was up in the air. How stupid could I be? Neither here or there should stupidity overrule me. This man called me asking a crazy question. "Does my daughter need anything for school?" He asked that proudly. How crazy can that be? After all, this is the same one that can dodge child support like a pro dodgeball player. I have never seen a man that could work a real job and the State is unable to find him for child support. And he has the nerve to brag to us about how he is living.

Anyway, my reply was "Huh?" After all, why would you ask a single parent with two teen daughters a crazy question like that? I felt like telling him, "We accept all methods of payments, Visa, MasterCard, American Express, Debit Cards, and EBT only to name a few. Our household does not discriminate with those who want to help." Once he determined that I was not in the mood for another disappointment he then asked for his daughter. I shall not tell a lie, my mind was cussing a hundred miles an hour but my lips were soft with,

"Hold on while I get her."

I scared myself with that response.

The spiritual growth in my life hasn't been a drastic change, but one that is continuous over time. It was apparent that I was changing because of my response to him. There is definitely a change in me. By now we would normally be fussing about me being the only one there all the time. You know how that conversation goes. Some of us can relate and agree that the same argument after a while can get old. This argument was almost full grown and really our tactics towards one another was not bringing about a change. One thing I have learned over the years is that you do not have to argue when you know that you are right. Although I wish that I could say that I learned this right away but I did not; I would be lying. This has taken practice and it will take more practice as long as I am human and will have to deal with another human being.

Since I was trying to enjoy the evening and only had my mind on the bubbles in the tub and a just a little peace of mind, I concluded that my piece of the conversation was finished. I called for my daughter to get the telephone and released the line. I usually will slowly release the phone line to see if I could listen in on the conversation to make sure that it was going according to my standards. However, this wasn't the time for me to be nosey and controlling. When you are the custodial parent you think you have to navigate everything and be in full and total control. She did not need me to talk to her father for her. That was something she was very capable of doing without my input.

It took God and everything that he put inside of me to change. My alter ego, "April" wanted to come out and make a pit stop with all of her baggage concerning my relationship with my child's father. Her (April's) bags were so full that Hefty was not tough enough to hold all of that crap. Sometimes analyzing yourself can be torture, but when I realized that I could make a difference in the situation that was once deemed as impossible to now being possible, then all was well.

This was the baby daddy that I skipped school with. The one that I knew would provide the love I that was seeking only to come up empty handed. He was the first someone that I thought truly cared, especially after I was pregnant with our child. For the longest time sex was love for me. I would often ask if I had put my life on hold for him. I was the one that was left raising our daughter and doing so the best that I knew how. The setbacks and situations in my life may have put certain things on hold, but I must remember that everything is part of the plan.

All a person needs sometimes is a listening ear and a helping hand and at times I thought he was incapable of either. Certainly this was a love-hate relationship. In one breath I could say that I loved him and the next exhalation I hated his guts.

'Do all baby mamas go through this?' If I answered for all of us, I would hear a corporate and resounding "yes". Now you can see why I love to escape to my homemade spa. It is refreshing to get away from it all and this night seems to be filled with more interruptions than what I would usually encounter.

Since this evening was not going as planned, my next move was to just go directly to bed and not even say goodnight to the girls. Taking my frustrations out on them would not solve anything. My kids knew me like a book. Whenever I would go through the house slamming cabinet doors and asking them to do ridiculous chores, they knew something was wrong.

Clearly this was not the night or the time for all of the foolishness that had occurred. These were minor storms on tonight, and each were coming one-by-one. Sometimes when it happens like this it could be catastrophic to one's thought process. You begin to think that you cannot deal with people or life for that matter. Well I have resolved to just rush my bath and go to bed and listen to my jazz. "Goodnight girls, I have had enough," I said.

Going to sleep was usually the easiest thing for me to do, but not *this* night. This night was unusual. It was typical for me to fall asleep without anything extra, as if I had my own personal anesthesiologist. Sometimes I believed myself to be a prime candidate of narcolepsy. But this night my mind began to wonder about the next day. I was thinking about what I was facing for the next day, I couldn't help but come to grips with a more pressing thought that my children had no clue what was going on with me.

This type of stuff is too heated for children and sometimes we cannot begin to explain our messed up lives to them. Do they understand? I think they do. It represented total embarrassment for me to tell my kids that my daddy, uncles, cousins and teachers all had me in a way that they should not have. People do not look at those that caused the hurt in your life, they only look at you and ask stupid questions, such as "why did you let them do this to you?" and "what kind of person are you?" People also make statements that are painful to the soul, such as "you must have liked it." To address that notion, I attest that I know the truth, and it is not my job to convince anyone that what I testify is total truth.

Anyway as I began to lay my head on my pillow I had to remember to "sleep pretty." We have two more days of this court stuff and my hairdo had to last for the rest of the week. Even though I knew this week was of pure hell and emotional torture, the diva side of me still took great pride in my appearance. While my little fingers reached for the remote to turn up the radio, this inner voice said to stop and pray. How can a saved woman stop and pray when an instrumental of Luther Vandross is playing?

An Intimate Night with God
My bed was lonely and praying was the furthest thing

from my mind. Since I did not have any potential boyfriends at this time, the closest that I was going to get to a man would be from the bible. This is an awful situation when you are lonely and you start to envision biblical men as fine. Some women feel as though they do not need men, but the truth is we need them just as much as they need us. Much conversation needed to take place between the Lord and I, therefore, I needed to confide in someone that I knew would listen and without passing judgment. This was a moment for me to stop what I was doing and listen to the voice of the Lord.

I have made so many mistakes in the past that making sure that it is his voice and not my own desires was difficult at times. That battle of knowing how to distinguish his voice from my own will or the devil's message was one that I mostly did not win. On many occasions my desires were so selfish that I would talk myself into believing that it was God instead of me. There are moments when it was confusing to decipher which voice to follow but from experience I recognized that his voice is calm and sweet. His voice is direct and not confusing. When I try to stray from what the Lord has spoken to me, He would often allow for a situation to lead me right back to what was originally purposed.

I quickly began to figure out that God is the final answer, and this did not come until after being hard-headed so many times. While in the past I had dismissed what God was saying to me, I was now growing to a new level of faith. I had cried, "God, I'm tired of this." My addiction to sex was turning into something that should've been sacred to me. The same way that some people are addicted to smoking, drugs, alcohol, gambling, and excessive spending, the evil one used the very thing that gives life to take mine away.

There were a lot of burdensome things on my heart that I needed to release once and for all.

> "Lord, please tell me what to do. I need you, Father. This has been a long week already. These next two days are going to be very hard for me. This is the part of my life that upsets my stomach. I do not like talking about those frightening times over at my Daddy's house. Lord, you were there when no one could testify for me and attest to the validity of my story. Lord, I need you to be with me at this time. People will be hurt about what is about to come forth, but you, Father, know my motive and my heart. You are the author of the Truth and know the truth of my life.
>
> You are my maker and know what is good for me. Can I truly make it through this? Will you be with me the next few days? Can I count on you

now? Do not leave me alone with these wolves, Father. They are seeking to scandalize my name and already have. They are looking to bring me to shame and make me feel that this is a worthless pursuit. I have vowed to always follow you. Since the birthing of my spirit and realizing that you live within me, Father, I have strived to recognize and obey your voice the best that I know how. My endeavor is to please you and not others. You are my Father and I hold you close to me Lord. I know you are a Spirit but since I have gone through so much, you have proven to be so much more in my life. I need you and I will hush to wait for your answer. You said in your Word that you would never leave me or forsake me. Please do not leave me now, for I need you in this darkest hour of my life. I need to feel your presence.

Sometimes I do not feel your presence and I am trying to believe that you are still there when I don't feel you or when I fail to see your works. Please be there for me so that I can be there for others. This whole thing is not for me, or even all about me. This is for other people to come out of bondage. They have to stop yielding to low self-esteem, loneliness and having a defeated spirit. I know they can, because You helped me realize the possibilities by walking me through it. There are many people, Lord, that do not know how to forgive others that have robbed them of their innocence and youthful hopes. I know that it's only by your Holy Spirit that I have matured. This is all that I have to say right now."

As I waited for his response the only thing that I heard was, "I love you." He said it so sweetly and forcibly that it shot like an arrow into my heart.

At about 3 o'clock I woke up and that inner voice told me to pray. I didn't have anyone on my prayer list and I was very sleepy. My flesh argued that it was too early to pray for anything. I wanted to go back to sleep. My pillow to the left of me was still cold. This sounds crazy but I like to flip my pillow over from time to time to feel the coldness of the other side touching my head. The thought of prayer this early in the morning wasn't going over too well for me. I needed a little more motivation.

A few minutes later this voice came again and said to pray. I started begging instead of praying. I was praying for strength. Then I threw in a little wealth and protection over my entire family. All of a sudden I started to pray for all of those who were out to harm me and tears began to fall from my eyes. I wondered, 'Why am I praying for my enemies that are known and unknown?' This is a weird feeling to pray for those who hurt you and misuse you. I said,

"Lord you know this is not an easy thing for me to do, and I couldn't really care any less about who needs prayer or that have done me wrong."

My pastor spoke about dealing with our giants a while back. In the bible, the story of David helps us to see that he couldn't have defeated the giant alone. He also needed help. It's the same as the giants that we face in our lives. God is there to help us just as he was there for David.

As I reflect on what my pastor taught us about the giants in our lives, I began to think about the giants in my very own life. Two of my giants were the incest and molestation. The third was love. I was very aware that these were the major giants in my life that had to be dealt with. When you have to stand against things that have more power than you would ever have, you become fearful. I am not afraid to say that I was fearful of coming forth and facing the criticism. For someone that did not mind fighting in school, this was a time that I felt that I had no more fight left in me. I was now facing giants that weren't afraid of my scare tactics. These giants seemed to not care that I was excelling in my studies or that I was trying to put on the face of being tough. These giants knew me better than I knew myself, and I know that I needed God's power to face them.

This was something that should still be under the rock. Hiding the fact that it ever happened is what got me through life. Did it really get me through life or was I trying to fake it until I made it? Once I finished praying, I was grateful that my notes were near. I started to search through my journal to go back over that lesson and read my notes and some scriptures from the bible. One scripture was that one from Philippians 4:13 which states, "I can do everything through Him that gives me strength." (NIV). That was a comforting scripture for me. Fear should not be in my vocabulary; better yet, it should not be my state of mind. Some things are much easier said than done, you know? Since I was filled with curiosity, reading the entire fourth chapter of Philippians was very comforting. By the time I looked over at the alarm clock there was only thirty minutes left to sleep.

Day 4:
"Pain in the Worst Way"

Since I was already up I thought to continue on with this day's activities. It was a little too early to wake up the girls; and especially my youngest daughter. She tries to get in all of the extra sleep that she can. It was like her sleep was on the auction block. Can I get a five more minutes over here or what about seven more minutes over there? I knew to just watch the news and tend to my morning routine before going to wake them up.

Just after hearing the traffic segment I usually free myself from 'the tube'. I must catch that segment along with the weather before heading to the shower so that I'll have an idea of what to expect before hitting the highway. As the water began to hit my back and I was crying out to the Lord the only reply I heard was,

> *"You'll be OK, I love you and I got your back. Don't worry about those things. I can handle it for you."*

My natural instinct was to start thinking that I was crazy. When you begin to experience the voice of the Lord it is a scary feeling. You want to openly share with others without them thinking that you are loony, but when you tell them that you hear a calm voice immediately they think you are crazy. You cannot share those experiences with everyone, because not all people are equipped to handle what is coming out of your mouth. I had to learn this the hard way. I began to hear this voice more frequently than in the past, and my thinking began to change, as well.

My morning was off to a great start and my oldest daughter swore up and down that she would be the one to get dressed first. We would make this a game and unfortunately, I would find myself being the loser many times. You would think that since I was up early that I could relax and not be rushed going out of the door. For the most part, my getting an early start really did not matter because I would take my time doing nothing.

As the morning departure time was growing near it dawned on me that once the kids went to school that this day was not going to be easy for me. I was playing it cool, but I started to break as we went out of the door. Tears began to come from my eyes and the kids began to wonder if they were the ones who had caused the sudden emotional change. They did not know that their mother was going to be emotionally slaughtered on the witness stand, but I did.

Since the tears were coming down like waterfalls with no end, I began to let them know that my emotional disturbance were not from anything that they have done. I told them, "I just want y'all to know that I love you and whatever goes on, you are loved."

Both of them nodded their heads in agreement that they understood. Usually they did not give me any trouble to make me cry, so the curiosity was high for them. They know that I am sensitive, but not like this. It was not time for me to tell them about my week in court and all that was going on with that.

This week had certainly been an act of therapy. As I proceeded down the highway my favorite morning show was on once again. This morning's discussion turned debate was about whipping your kids or giving them time out. The show's audience is very urban. Some of us that listen are so out-of-the-box with our responses. Do you ever respond to the airwaves? My answer was to spank that fanny. Most of the people that listen in our communities are in agreement that corporal disciplining of our children when necessary is very acceptable. We often take the Malcolm X approach, and by that I mean, by any means necessary, a parent has to do what a parent has to do. It's either discipline them or allow them to experience destruction. I believe in discipline, but I do not believe in abuse. There is a big difference!

I wanted to get to the courthouse a little early to eat breakfast because the food in my opinion was delicious! Eating before getting back on the witness stand will give me enough strength to handle the series of events.

Before entering into the courtroom I went to the bathroom to pray.

> "Lord, give me the strength to withstand all negative thoughts, critical actions and lies that may come my way. Help me not to sway and hide because this is a time of healing, and a time of truth. Lord, give me the boldness to want to stand up and stand out to help others that are in the same situation or that could relate to my experiences. I know that my life is not about me, exclusively, but about others. Lord I need you to guide me to be that great steward over my life, family, my finances and all that come in contact with me for guidance and support. Thank you Lord for I know that you hear all of my prayers and that this is done. In Jesus name I pray, Amen."

I began to walk into the courtroom and my eyes were already filled with tears. That was because of the intimate talk that I had with my Father. I saw more familiar faces again. My mother and grandmother were there. This was difficult for me because it was people that I loved that did not know about half of the stuff that happened to me. I have to remember that this testimony is beyond me. It extends beyond my family and reaches those who can relate this story. This is about God's will and his purpose for my life and the lives of others who are seeking a release from the prison walls of sexual abuse.

"Ms. Zanderson will you please take your seat in the witness stand?"

"Sure, Judge," I replied and I went to the stand with a little more confidence than I had felt from the days before mainly because of all the prayers that led up to now.

As I began to sit down I heard a voice from the audience yell, "You're trying to destroy us." My instructions were precise on how to handle such matters and that is what is taking place right now.

The judge spoke to me,

"Ms. Zanderson, please pick up where we left off on yesterday evening."

Pain, Torture and Hell

"Well, as I can remember this was the time when all confusion was in my mind. I only had a few days more to live with my grandmother. The abortion was completed and I was still sick and devoid of feelings.

The only person that I could live with was my daddy. The time was growing near where removing me from the home was not my choice, but that of the law's, since they were now involved. This detective made me leave my granny's house and go live with my dad. We packed up all my clothes and off I went. This was such an interesting and yet most dysfunctional part of my life. I was a teen going through a part of my life that had so many unanswered loopholes and many silenced solutions. When I arrived at my dad's house, there was a woman there with three little girls. The girls' ages ranged from about three through seven.

When I saw the little girls, I could only help but wonder if these girls were being abused just as I was. I did not forget what happened to me; nor the physical abuse that he caused to my mother and his previous wives. I figured that his girlfriend was either happy to have a man or pleased to leave the environment she was accustomed to. She did not have to work, but she had so many other responsibilities that it was sickening to watch her just bow down to him like that. She was very nice to me, but she was a person who portrayed low self-esteem because she did everything that he asked her to do. I guess that's what a woman is supposed to do, right? He treated her nice by taking her to the store to buy clothes and groceries. I always thought that he went for the weaker woman who would stay home while he went out and did God knows what. He thought that he was a modern day Casanova.

I really felt sorry for her because he would only do just enough to keep her there and my little teen-aged eyes couldn't comprehend that a true love may have existed beyond what I saw.

The children did not have anything in common with me because they were always in the bed or in their room as punishment for doing something wrong. My summer events seem to be turning for the worse.

The detective came by the house a few days later and began to talk to my dad. Through his investigation he wanted to know my point of view. However, he never asked me anything in front of my dad. Since I was a minor, one of my parents would have to make the decision to press charges, at least this is what I believed. This was the time that my daddy wanted to step up to his "fatherly responsibilities". I knew that this man had a conscience, speaking of my dad. He must've and just did not express to us that he really was a *sane* individual. My dad started the process and the investigator said that it would be a couple of days and he would get back with him.

A couple of days turned into a week which really seemed like a month. During these days we experienced a lot of solemn moments in that household.

My daddy never did apologize to me for touching me

and also having me one night at his mother's house when I was a little girl. It was like he didn't care, or maybe he thought that I had forgotten the incident. Perhaps this was just a slip of his mind and it really did not happen, at least in his mind. Even if he had forgotten, I surely could not forget! I'm the one that has to live with this and contend with all of these issues. The only thing that my memory would reflect on is that he had messed with me, too. While there in the home with him and his girlfriend and her children, I would think to myself that these little girls may have gone through the same thing. Once a man can go there with his own daughter he can also do it to others with no conscience at all!

The few weeks that I was there felt like a living hell. I did not have any friends over where he lived. He was always mean and wanted to try to whoop me for anything possible. I always felt his anger. He was a *very* angry man. Everything at that time was his way or no way at all. Never did he show me what it was like to have a father that I could talk to. You know, the kind of man that you would like to compare your boyfriend to? Well this was not it. I was afraid of him because of how I had seen him treat people in the past. Many times I would think that it was because he did not like my mother that he hated me so much.

When the investigator came back to give the information about pressing charges against my uncle the news must have reversed. From the events that I am about to tell you, I was able to read between the lines and figure out that my dad had been found out! My mom was out of town and he came to me about the incident that my mom reported. The situation was really bigger than me and too much for my little shoulders to carry.

My daddy started cussing and looking at me with fire in his eyes. He wanted to know, when did we have the time to report the information to the courts? He had no clue that my mother had begun to report the incident of him touching me inappropriately. I told him that I thought that he knew what was going on. My mother started the process, but until this day I really do not know what happened with that case. He was so mad at her, and also at me. I was very confused, I didn't know what to do and I just knew that he was going to beat me up. I was not going to get just a regular whipping, but an actual fight. I have seen him put his fists on other women, and I believed wholeheartedly that he was going to do the same thing to me!

That entire day I was called everything but a daughter of God. I was every bad woman that a cussing sailor could think of. He tortured me verbally and gave me the nastiest attitude that I could've ever imagined. This went on the whole day.

That night felt like the torment from hell. I wanted to believe that visiting hell may have even been better than what I was facing. This was an agonizing evening. His girlfriend was there along with her kids when all of this went on. He made them stay away from me like I had some type of plague or something. They did not know any better so they did exactly as he instructed them to do. It was like living under a dictatorship and he was the master dictator.

This evening is one that I would never forget. I was literally tortured. By him being so mad at me for every little thing and the fact that he found out that there was a case against him did not make it any better. He made me suffer the most horrific night of my life. I could remember him cussing me out and making me lie on the floor.

Now we went to bed very early on this night. The entire household was in the bed right at sunset. His girlfriend and I were in the same room with him. He made me lie down on a pallet on the floor. All of the lights were out in the house no one moved and we could hardly breathe. I was crying and slinging snot all over the place. The louder that I cried the worse he would get. My dad said things like, "you told on me and said I did things now I'm going to show you."

Sometime past midnight as the morning approached, he went to his car and got out this bat that he normally had under the driver's seat of the car. When he came back in the house he was hitting the bat in his hand as if it was lights out for one of us. He pranced around and cussed all evening long. He would come close to my head with the bat and pranced up and down the room for hours. His girlfriend was there and was more afraid of him than I was. She did not have enough in her to try to take up for me.

Now one thing that he did know and would say about me is I had a smart mouth. I knew how to stand up for myself, but this time I was up against a losing battle so I had thought. Again, he came close to me with the bat and would get so close as if he was going to beat my brains out. I was crying but could not cry that loud because I knew that in a moment it could be over for me.

I began to pray silently and the prayer went something like this,

> "Lord, if you just let me make it out alive I won't turn back. If you hear me Lord, please help me. You know that I'm telling the truth. Help me God."

I really did not know to what extent these words helped the situation. The prayer was one that was short but had a lot of validity to it. The torture seemed liked it lasted for days. I was in a desperate situation and needed someone to come and rescue me. I could not call for anyone, and the one person that could take a stand did not. It boggles my mind to think of how his girlfriend was of no help and I could only wonder, what was she there for. How could I expect for her to save me when she could not save herself? He just had his way with me that night. I could not cry and it seems like every step he made the bat was getting closer to my head. Once I saw that he wasn't going to kill me, then I was relieved. Then he took me into the living room.

My dad knew that he started molesting me at an early age and then he pretended that he didn't remember any of it. When he took me to the living room I was still praying silently and hoping that God heard me. I was asking for a way out. My dad put me on the couch and had his way with me. He went beyond the point of fondling me, this was truly a sexual encounter. I remember him saying,

"Since y'all say I did it - then I will!"

He knew the whole time that he did all of those horrific things to me, and that everything I reported was the truth! He did things to me that daddy's do not do to their daughters!

Although he didn't beat me that night, tears ran down my face uncontrollably and he threatened that if I did not stop crying he was going to hit me. As real as everything was to me, still, I couldn't understand why and how he could do such things. And watching this man lose his mind with me was her... his girlfriend. While I was in my own struggle to live through this night, I still mustered up the consideration to think about her and her daughters. I thought that if he could do that to me, then certainly he would do it to her and her children. I remember saying to her (in my mind), 'you should not want to stay with someone that has mental issues such as this.' Or, better yet, 'how could you live in the house with a man knowing what he just did to his daughter?'

The next morning came, and to my surprise, he hugged me like nothing ever happened. He didn't even apologize. Just this weird "fatherly" type of hug that accompany a scripture quote in hopes that I wouldn't judge him for the nightmare he authored. I never judged him; more like *hated* him for allowing the wicked forces to come in and use him to destroy my life.

I could not wait until my mother came to pick me up. She did not know what I was going through before she got there. I thought that there was no use in telling her when no one cared anyway. That summer I felt like a female David from the Bible. I was a murderer, homeless, violated, crazy and anything else that was negative it fell upon me and I was expected to deal with it. My esteem was so low and my mentality was so off." I spoke up,

> "Judge can we please stop for today and pick up tomorrow? I can't take anymore!"

> *"Ms. Zanderson you're doing very well, and yes we can resume in the morning at 8:30am. We should be here only half the day tomorrow. Court is adjourned."*

"A Moment of Relief"
I ran out of the courtroom and not to the restroom, but to the cafeteria. My "mood food" was calling me...French fries! I rushed down and ate a basket full of fries with plenty of ketchup and a large cola. This was the type of meal that calmed my nerves and could satisfy any tension that I had to temporarily deal with. I had a lot to think about and actually up until this time, I did not want to relive this tragedy. Leaving the courthouse was a relief for me. This day was the hardest of them all. Out of all days, this one was the worst to remember.

This part of my story is one that I dreaded to tell. For years it was only a select few that I was able to share this trauma with. I believe that those people were chosen by God so that they too would realize that they are not alone. It was commendable that I was able to stand before a crowd and let it all out. Sharing with the whole world that my father was sexually abusive and having me as if I were some woman on the streets was so embarrassing. But having the courage to tell the truth was liberating all at the same time.

I needed to hear some Gospel music. My CD collection was limited, but track that I wanted to hear was already in the CD player. "In The Midst of It All," was playing and it gave me much hope and encouragement. I could only wave my hands and began to tell the Lord, "thank you;" thank you for all that I have experienced and gone through.

As I started to fuss with the people in traffic, that voice came to me again, "I love you. You are special to me." This was only the Lord letting me know how he felt about me. My reassurance came quite frequently lately. He only wanted me to know that all was well, and that he was there for me.

This day may have been difficult to deal with, but it was certainly a relief for me. After reliving this I felt as though I could conquer anything that was set before me. The hard part was over. That is what I thought. Once you have had the man who was chosen to take care of you to do you in, you feel doomed. My life was heading to the pits of hell... or so I thought.

Besides fries and music, another measure of therapy for me was shoe shopping. Since I had some time before the kids were out of school, I decided that I needed some therapy, and stopping over to look for some shoes always proved to be soothing to me.

I went to my favorite joint where you could find all kinds of "foot fun," for all women with various tastes in shoes. Let me tell you, I became like a child in a candy store. "Fortunate" was my middle name because on this fortunate day I walked into a Super Sale. The shoes were marked down to their lowest price. My day at court triggered this spree, but this was a way for me to deflect from the emotions that I have to currently deal with. I was looking up and down the aisles with greed in my eyes, not wanting another soul to buy any available pair of shoes. I wanted them all for myself. Selfish? Yes, but it was true. Needless to say, I came out of the store with ten pairs of shoes. I was happy, indeed.

Shopping was right up my alley, and it was Thursday, and there was an automatic deposit that would post to my bank account in the afternoon. I had it going on and was only taking applications for future haters. You couldn't tell me anything. The shoes brought a smile to my face, but when I got in the car, it hit me. Not the amount that was spent, but the fact that I had to share my shoes with my girls. Even when I would tell them no, they would try to find a way for me to say yes.

It was Baby-Girl that was the first to be picked up on today. She was so glad to see me, too! Things had not gone well for her, and my cell phone was off due to court rules. She had tried to reach me, which proved impossible. She had one of those days that girls try to avoid when our boyfriends are involved. Now, remember that I was already an emotional wreck. However, I was pacified through shoe therapy. She needed me and unfortunately I was not available. The last thing that I wanted to do was transfer negative energy to her.

As soon as she got in the car, she didn't say that she missed me. The first thing to come out of her mouth was,

> "You won't believe what happened to me today. The nerve of that boy! He tried to go out with my best friend. He had us arguing over nonsense, him. This has been my friend since the third grade, and fighting over some boy was not my M.O."

I looked over at her to see if that was my daughter talking. She asked me,

> "What am I to do? I like my boyfriend and my best friend, and he is in the middle of it all."

My advice to her was to stick with your friend. Friends

to the end and boys will come and go. Your friend will be with you for a long time. Your job is to be friends with both of them. I stated that she should treat him fairly, but tell him that he cannot be a player and expect for her to play nice. She said that she would take my advice and let me know how things went the next day.

We had to hurry up to finish with this conversation because her older sister was about to enter in the car. I knew exactly when we should share information and when it was off limits to the other family members. Normally we did not keep secrets from one another, but I had to respect the fact that the both of them had boundaries, and this was one of those times.

When my oldest daughter got into the back seat of the car, she could sense that we were up to something. She wanted to know what was going on and after we didn't respond, she went on to tell us about her day. Her day was seemingly normal and no "hallway gossip" as she would refer to her juicy events. She did mention that one of the teachers upset her to the point of her having an attitude. This teacher made her very upset that it was difficult for her to explain to me why she was reprimanded. She began talking so fast we thought she was speaking another language. I allowed her the moment to get it all out so that she would feel better. We certainly felt a sigh of relief because she began to sound like herself again. Our famous question that we address every evening was presented. "What's for dinner?" 'That was a magical question that could not be answered.

I did tell them,

"I'm not cooking tonight."

"I'll cook," yelled my youngest daughter.

We knew that we were going to have hot dogs, Sloppy Joes or Hamburger Helper. This was the Hamburger Helper night because I did not feel the cooking thing and knew that they had to have something nutritious. Just because I choose not to cook all the time does not mean that they could not join in to make a decent meal.

I made sure that our household was definitely balanced, and I proved it by insisting that each one of us made an honest and fair contribution. Everyone carried their own weight and then some.

My oldest daughter had to do more than the youngest, and that was to be expected. You know there's always a mother figure among siblings and my oldest daughter is the mother hen. Much responsibility was put upon her because I had to work and take care of them to the best of my ability. So we decided to let the youngest make dinner, and she had about two hours to give us our evening feeding.

Everyone was excited when we got home because it was "Throwback Thursday" on our local radio station. It was a joy to see my children appreciating the music that I grew up listening to. We formed a Soul Train line right in my living room, and it was on in the dance arena. Any way that I can get my children to be active is a plus, and we all love to dance. We got in that house and threw on our house clothes which consisted of long T-shirts and old scrub pants and old oiled up head scarves that we all raced to get into so that we could be comfortable. Never do we look like the person that others see at work or school.

Everyone decided to disperse to their room after dinner was served, but I knew that I would have to coerce one of them to go out and get the shoes from my car. I was ecstatic because this week had drained me mentally and emotionally, and I would need some type of project to distract me from what I was feeling on the inside. Why not take advantage of this time and pair shoes with outfits...sounds perfect to me!

> "I really wished one of my daughters loved me well enough to go out to get my shoes out of the trunk," I hinted.

They both looked at me as if to say, 'She always asks us to go back out when we have gotten comfortable.'

The frustrated looks on their faces did not bother me because I knew what was in the trunk. They had not a clue. Oh, but when they saw how many were in the bags, they would want a piece of the action. I knew that picking out shoes with their outfits would keep them occupied while I went to my room for some "me" time. Even though I could hide all that was going on from the children from an emotional standpoint, inside it was a derailment. This was the perfect time for me to sit and pray as well as listen to my Father.

"Father, once again I am here before you this week. This week I seem to be before you more times than others. You know exactly what I am going through. You were there when I wanted to just bump each one of them off, one-by-one. This may be hard for you to listen to Father with me talking about killing your children and all, but they did me wrong. I know you've seen and heard all of it. Help me, Dear Father, to truly forgive those who have hurt me and caused so much pain. Help me to tolerate and love those who could not even say that they were sorry. Lord, only you know how much I can truly take. You made me in your perfect form, but my ways are so imperfect.

My thoughts are definitely not yours, Father, and I need you right now. Speak to me so that I can continue to follow your rules and your pathway. Sometimes I do not know if what I say at times is appropriate, but it is from the heart, and it is real. Comfort me, Oh Lord, and put your loving arms around me. Hold me in your arms and protect me from those that wish to do me harm. Please love me the way a Father should and allow me to experience the greatness of a Father's love. Let me see that you're there for me when I'm not even there for myself. Allow me to have the opportunity to feel your presence. I want to be used by you God, and do your will. Come into my heart right now and renew my heart, my mind, and my Spirit. I want what you want for me Oh God. Help me to see that this journey thus far is not about me but about others that need you. Let me be a light in the midst of darkness. You know my faults and my weaknesses, and I am the first to admit that I need help.

You are always there for me, and many times I fall, but I know that you will help me get up and back onto my path. Lord, help me to know where I stand with you and that these matters of the heart that I share with you, stand as an agent that will strengthen our bond. I am not a preacher or a savior, but I am a servant. You have helped me, so please allow me the opportunity to serve in the areas that you find me most qualified. If I cannot do anything else in this life Lord, allow me to be a great servant. This too shall pass. This week will pass. The bad memories will pass. The embarrassment will pass. The moments of unbelief about my future will pass. One more thing Lord, please forgive me for all of the hatred that is harbored in my heart and in my mind. Tomorrow is the last day of this trial, and then the weekend. I need peace and calmness in my life. Any storm that comes my way - please allow me the strength to overcome. Lord, you are my Father, friend, and comforter. I love you and ask that you continue to mold me to be the woman that you set out for me to be. Thank you for listening to me, Lord.

Please protect the children that you have given me to raise to become decent young women. They were loaned to me by you, and I thank you for that. Help me to be a great steward of all that you blessed me with. I now close and ask all of these things in your son Jesus Christ name. Amen."

By the time I finished talking to my Father I was in my dark room just thinking and listening. I heard that calm voice assuring me that He loves me and that He will always be there. It's moments like these that get me through.

The girls knew it was my quiet time and did not bother me. Once the door opened, I was greeted with hugs, and that always made me feel on top of the world. It's good to know that loving arms are available when you need them. So far, this week has been a whirlwind of emotions and filled with tons of mommy duties; but with God's help and the presence of my children, I was confident that I could handle the next day in court. I knew if the girls and I could just have that time to wind down, then I can mentally prepare for what's to come.

The girls wanted to watch a chick-flick, so we did. We loved this goofy movie that really touched our little hearts. This particular movie inspired us to be hopeful and allowed us to see that anything is possible. Some of the scenes provided so much laughter with the goofiness and costumes. "B.A.P.S." will forever be watched in our family. Sometimes I wished that we didn't watch it so much because my daughters have moments where they recite lines, so much so that it becomes annoying.

With much laughter and an ambiance of candles and buttered microwave popcorn, I will say that this evening is chilled and relaxed. Mind you, they haven't forgotten about the shoe rampage that I went on. So in between scenes, we were piecing our outfit for the next day. The youngest one said that she was going to rock those heels the next day at school. I laughed because going up and down school hallways in high heel shoes is murder to one's feet. She should have learned from her older sister that heels and halls do not mix. I can rock those heels because they come off when I am sitting at my desk, and that is how I make it through the day.

Usually, I am the first one to fall asleep during a movie, and sometimes it's a struggle for me to make it through the entire movie, so there's no sense in changing up now. When this happens, my children flip the script and tell me to go to bed. This would not have been the first time that I was summoned to go to bed. My oldest daughter always seemed to take charge when she saw an opportune time to do so. Off to bed I went like I was their child. They did not have to tell me twice or even get an argument out of me. The day was long and too many things were on my mind. Trying to get my mind emotionally stable for tomorrow was an event all by itself.

I thought that listening to classical music while in bed would do me some good and change my mood or at least ease the thoughts that were racing from the left and right side of my brain. Even the classical music wasn't of any help. After a while, the strings and percussions seemed to be getting on my nerves. I decided to turn on the television after being in much discontent. What do you know? I woke up to the TV being on a religious station and unfortunately this message wasn't working for me either. Since nothing seemed to appease me during the wee hours of the morning, I thought to put in one of my tapes from church service that will allow me to cosign the pastor with an "amen" and "that's right" throughout the message. I began listening to a message entitled "You Could Never Fall."

I started to listen to the message and tears began to fall from my face because some of the points really hit home. The only thing that I could meditate on is the fact that failure was not an option. Falling is given to all and when you fall you can still get up. God created us with life and with the ability to stand when faced with adversities and not to lie down and give up during hardships. Rising was in my spirit and shining was in my soul, but with the next morning's events embedded in my mind, it was difficult to stay high-spirited. However, I found something from within that allowed me to rise above the circumstances and push my way through this week.

This week was certainly one to be remembered. It was almost over and knowing that this morning was the last day of my testimony helped me and that was a *huge* relief. Now, getting back to sleep was impossible with visions and thoughts racing in my mind, but I found a way to nod off. It was not too soon after the nod that the alarm on my cell phone went off. I have been up in the wee hours of the morning, tossing and turning, watching and listening, and still an emotional wreck because of regurgitating my past.

I turned the television back on expecting to hear some good news, and that was a joke on me, especially when the local news is so predictable.

Day 5:

"Victorious After the Pain"

The typical morning in our household is busy and unorganized. My children were up stirring around with all the lights on, every radio up and radio stations colliding with one another, along with the television playing. Too much noise and chaos seem to be a normal routine for us in the mornings. We try to combat our chaos with preparation and to which any efforts put in the night before is null and void by morning. We will pick outfits out and have them ironed and still change our minds. God forbid if one of us is having a B.H.D. (bad hair day). This was one of those mornings for me. I just could not seem to get my hair to cooperate, or pick out the right shoes to wear. After going on a shoe shopping rampage the day before, that really brought more confusion to the household. Since it is the last day that I was to appear before the judge, my threads had to be together. Finally, they were.

Now that I have the girls out of the car and I can concentrate on making my way to the courthouse. I anticipated that the traffic would be light since we had to leave out a little early. Needless to say, all was going well until I got on the service road. It doesn't take much for a person to have road rage in this city.

How can you get mad at someone that can't move? Easily, we do it every day in life, and not just in traffic jams or signal lights. We have the nerve to get mad at our friends and family when they are not moving at the speed we want them to. We become furious with our loved ones when they do not move at all.

It dawned on me that this is the same way we allow people to enter in our minds and then hinder our lives. We play victim all too well with one another. We pick up other people's problems and swear up and down that they caused us to react in such a way. No, we caused the reaction because we decided to tackle something that was not assigned to us; which is other people's problems.

While I was inching my way through this traffic, I heard that inner voice again. It reassured me once more that everything was going as expected and that I was going to be okay. For once in my life, belief was on a total high. I believed in that inner voice telling me that all is well and it felt wonderful. I could go into the courthouse with a smile on my face because being ashamed was no longer one of my bags I had to carry. There was a lot that had to be covered in such a short time, and it was worth it. Thoughts were being tossed around in my mind like a strong current, but this had to be done. I had to tell all of my story; once and for all.

I said a quick prayer,

"Not my will Lord, your will be done. This is not about me, but it is about you and your glory. You would not have brought me this far to leave me alone to face the enemy. Give me strength and wisdom on this day and going forward. I know that you are God and God alone, so help me to be all that you have purposed for me to be. Thank you, and I love you, Lord".

I didn't have any regrets pulling into the courthouse parking lot today. Finally, my side of the story was out and therefore I can now move forward. You do not know my story the way I know it and have lived it. The only other someone that can truly attest that everything is true in my eyes and in His eyes is my heavenly Father. I thank Him for being omniscient, all knowing.

I traveled through downtown smiling like I had just won the lottery. Sometimes, when things have burdened you for so long, it seems like there is never light at the end of the tunnel. At this very moment, I felt richer than rich and tangible hope for a wealthy and healthy state of mind.

As I walked through the courtroom doors my heart was light; lighter than it had ever been taking this familiar path. I was ready to get to the stand because I knew that it was almost over. The courtroom was not as crowded today as the previous days this week. I have never been so spoiled.

This was an unusual trial because the judge was always waiting for me. No matter how early or late that I was, I figured it was my show starring me. I took the witness stand, and he proceeded by asking me to pick up from the day before. In my mind, I was thinking that he had to be on something very potent to expect for me to perform a miracle like that. I could hardly remember what happened this final morning, but if he would ask a leading question that would be helpful. At one point, I began to stare up at the ceiling, and he asked,

> *"What happened when your mother came to get you?"*

I responded,

> "Well, my mother came to get me the next day and it was perfect timing. I had just encountered the worst night of my entire life up until that time. My daddy just had me in the worst way and was thinking of killing me, and I had been left defenseless. I was thinking, 'why did they have me?' He was just so mean and unkind toward others and cared only for himself. That night proved that he didn't care about me. He only cared about himself and trying to make

the truth out to be a lie.

My mother loved me in her own special way. She was probably confused because my grandmother stepped in to raise me, and probably thought that she didn't have a voice in my life. She did the best that she could do with me, and I love her for that. She had to take a lot of knocks upside the head (literally) for me. I can say that when I needed things for school or clothes she managed to get the money for it. How she got the money? That really wasn't my business, only a secondary concern of mine. For all the sorrow she caused or allowed, I knew she went to the lengths that she could go to be the best that she could be.

This is one of the times that I truly needed her to protect me and to be there for me. She came to pick me up, and my daddy did not tell her anything about what he did to me. I did not tell her because I was ashamed. How could the same man that had a part in conceiving me also violate me? This was puzzling, and that question still grips me at certain times in my life. It is hard to forget what someone has done to you. I often hear others say, 'you have to bury that stuff-just forget about it.' Usually, the ones that give this type of advice are the same ones that hold on to any and everything in their life, as well. For instance, you can forgive your mother for whipping you, but you never forget the sting she left on the backside. To forgive is one thing and to forget is totally another.

I was kind of excited to live with her because I could not remember just the two of us living together alone. I have always desired that she and I live together and for our bond as mother and daughter to strengthen. I was told that if you hold on to your dreams, that one day that they would come true. Well, this one finally did, despite the circumstances. We packed all of my stuff in the car, and I departed with my mother.

My daddy was happy to see me leave and the feelings were mutual on my part. I could not tell my mother what went on. I did not know what to do or say. I just came out of this thing with my uncle, and now my own daddy tried to kill me after having his way with me sexually. This was too embarrassing and also painful. I wondered if anyone in this world could be going through this. I was scarred for a long time.

My mother was just settling in her new town with a new job, and now she had a teenager on her hands. A teenager that has been damaged and traumatized from being sexually abused. I didn't care where my mother decided to take me as long as I didn't have to deal with what I had just come through. She was living in a hotel room temporarily until she was able to find a permanent place to live. My mom decided to make the west her home. She was still getting acquainted with her boyfriend's relatives and friends and new job, and I don't think she was ready for all that I had come with.

The little town that she now called home was totally opposite of the big city that we both had come from. I did not see how I was going to find a new normal. I might as well make the best of the situation because this was where I would be attending school this year.

My whole world was new, and I had a lot of adjusting to do. We were doing fine, and as time went by, we started to understand each other a little better. She had her moments too. I was feeling a little secure and thought that this was the coolest thing – for mom and me to finally get the opportunity to live together alone. It was going fine until they started drinking. They started to argue and fight like children. That is the one thing that a child should not have to experience. I had experienced direct abuse and again indirect abuse concerning my mother. I had to see her hurt physically, emotionally, mentally, and verbally. All the forms of abuse that anyone could imagine, she has endured. I think my eyes have seen a little bit too much as well as my body experiencing too much physical trauma.

I prayed, "Please Lord make them stop fighting." They would cuss each other out, and when you first heard it, you would think that a fight was coming instantaneously. This was the norm, so I was confused. It was difficult for me to decipher if it was the alcohol talking or their way of communicating. They knew the difference but I did not and therefore I figured that it was best that I stay out of their affairs because once all the drama cleared they were back to being best buddies.

It hurt me to see my mother go through things such as this. When you see your mother get slapped down to the ground and kicked around just on GP (general principle), that isn't good. She is not a dog and should not be knocked to the ground. In one incident, I remembered him hitting her, and every time she tried to get up, he would hit her again. Why didn't I help her? I couldn't. She did not allow me to get in the middle of their affairs. They would fight and then make up on the same day, or maybe even the next day and things for them were back to normal.

The semester that I spent in high school in west Texas could not go by fast enough. This was a new town and I had to make friends all over again. Even though I experienced everything about sex before my time, the act of love still remained unseen. I didn't know how to love anyone. How could I love someone when loving me seems to be impossible? I thought I was ugly because boys would tell me so. The male species should have been the furthest thought from my mind with all that had occurred, but for some reason, they were not. I felt the need to make it a personal mission of mine to keep looking for love in all the wrong places, cracks, and crevices because I longed for something that I never experienced, and that is a genuine love. I was not considered as being 'hot as a firecracker' as most would think or want to believe, but I definitely had some issues going on. However, I felt as if I were more like a lonely dove. It was really sad because it was not to my advantage to be this way.

I had to get acclimated to the changes that this move and town had to offer. I had to grow accustomed to what this high school had to offer. It was very diverse in culture and very much westernized; I mean country and western. All you saw were Roper boots and Wrangler jeans and some grown adult looking child with a mouth full of tobacco. However, I was fortunate to make acquaintance with some of the upper classmen. I met two wonderful young ladies that had moved from Louisiana to west Texas, and boy were they a fun pair to be around. They were driving and hanging out and partying with the upperclassmen because they fit into that group. One was a junior and the other a senior, and I- I was the unpopular freshman trying to gain points wherever possible.

They exposed me to football games, drinking and partying, and I thought this was the best thing ever. Since I was not blessed to have the name brand clothes growing up, I considered it a privilege to be around those who did. This was certainly a way for me to rise on the popularity charts. The only thing that was going well for me at the time was my figure, and that was bringing more harm than good. Once you have been engaging in any sexual activity whether you wanted it or not, it is devastating to a young, immature body. I began to love what wasn't good for me and did not know how to quit. There was popular new drug campaign (Just Say No) encouraging young people to stay away from drugs, should have also applied to sex. The worries of being molested or even raped left my mind because I knew there was not anyone there to bother me, which left me with a feeling of security.

This was because I knew that mom's boyfriend was just mean and crazy, but not sexually drawn towards me. I also knew you could never be too sure of people and their underlying motives. The new move and school were coming along very well, and I was adjusting to the climate of a little city in west Texas.

I guess things were going just a little too good for me because one day my mother got out of her head and approached me with, "I guess you want him too. You already had everybody in the family." She probably didn't realize what she had said. To this day, I never brought it to her attention. When a person is under the influence anything is liable to roll off their tongue. Over the years I had to learn to let it go. I also learned that alcohol would have its partakers doing and saying things that they normally wouldn't do. Why is all hell breaking loose in my life? The hurdles were becoming difficult it seemed like every day. It seems like everyone around me was against me. My world was closing in on me. Love, peace, joy and self-control were only a dream to me. I felt that I wasn't deserving to have any of these virtues.

This is just what the enemy wanted. The enemy is the author of confusion so his mission to break the bond between and mother and daughter would be right up his sleeves. Who could I turn to during this difficult time? I thought this was the great escape from all of the chaos I had left behind, but evidently not. The lyrics from "Go to the Rock" came to mind. Where do I go? Who do I turn to? My options were getting to be slim to none. My mother was the only person that I could live with and didn't have anyone else that I could've reached out to.

I just could not take this anymore. It was getting ridiculous. The Lord only puts on you what you can handle. This was becoming unimaginable because my load was too heavy and I was only a teenager. My troubles were supposed to fit an adult - someone who has the shoulders to carry all of this mess. This was the worst time in my life. Still, I somehow made it through. I returned to live with my grandmother after being with my mother for few months, and the cycle stopped for a while. But eventually, it started all over again in another form. The baggage that I had to tote left me with desiring love, but in the form of sex.

Once I moved back, no one messed with me for a long time and this was because of all of the events that were occurring. For example, I was older, and there had been a few months lapse since my life-altering abortion. The months after that went by so fast and numerous things had occurred. As I mentioned before, I have a mental block about things that took place during my sophomore year of high school. I could remember a few of my teacher's faces but not their names, and only a few classmates from high school. This was a vicious cycle that I knew must stop. Thank goodness that eventually it did.

I went back home to try to live a normal life, but everything was different. I was able to block out things that happened when in the company of others, but inside I was a total wreck of emotions. Hatred! Hatred! Hatred set in, and then the plot to kill every man that touched me was consistently on my mind, and I knew that was wrong. How did I deal with this? It was not easy, and it took a long time afterward to get to the heart of the matter. I was really hurt by not getting the support from my mother when I really needed her. No matter what she did for me as a baby, including bringing me into this world, that one accusation really made the difference in our relationship.

It took all of this hell to make me the woman I am today, and now, Judge, I can say that the understanding is greater and the love for God is immensely great, and there is no other love I would rather have. This is it, Judge. This is all that I have to say."

"Well done, you may leave the witness stand now."

The people in the courtroom were left speechless with all of the things that occurred in my life from a toddler up until the age thirteen - which actually stretched to sixteen. My life didn't appear to be in shambles for those who were on the outside looking in. I learned how to hide my feelings and true emotions. I hid everything that was happening to me, and quite naturally this was becoming the norm - hiding the things that shouldn't be hidden. Actually, I thought that what I was experiencing was the norm and that most young girls my age were going through the same things. This day in court was special to me because finally, someone took out time to listen to me.

My plans for the upcoming weekend were not filled with much scheduled activity, but I was looking forward to enjoying myself. As I was leaving the courthouse tears of joy came rolling down. I had survived the storm. This storm was internal and had lasted for so many years. There's nothing like going through a storm that no one else can see or feel, but you. What's unique about these types of storms is, you're the only one who is able to recognize when the sunshine has returned again, and you're the only one that can feel God's umbrella of protection upon the current situation.

We read about the woman in the bible with an issue of blood and how long it took for her to be healed; a whole twelve years! I really had some issues that no one could seem to solve. They were deep and buried underneath all of these layers. It's finally over. The pain, the weight, the burden of keeping silent- it's finally over! What is the antidote? Where did I go from here?

It was Friday, and the Judge didn't mention when the verdict would be read. Since we did not have a definite date as to when we would resume with everything, I was going to party. My kids were going over to their father's house for the weekend, and I knew that I had the opportunity to let go and live it up. I decided to get the car washed so I would not have to ride dirty. Now that I just bought all those shoes, a new outfit was soon to follow, and this evening was it. My hair was still looking good, and I had my nails done, but the new outfit was missing. I knew once the kids were picked up I could head down to our local fashion spot and find something that wasn't too expensive, but definitely presentable for a night out on the town. It had to be casual and sophisticated with just a little pizzazz. Just my kind of style!

Finally, my side of the story was told, and everyone that speculated as to what went on (and for those who were right up under my nose that didn't have a clue) were duly informed. I knew that after this week there would be a lot of people with strong opinions. Some of those that I thought were true friends and loved me would later turn against me. The individuals that knew that all of this was going on and did not say or do anything were shocked. They never knew that the other side of the coin was finally flipped. The faces of many people dropped and I was free, and the idea of celebrating was just circling in my brain. I even started to sing "Celebration" knowing that it was my time to rejoice for my freedom was here.

You would've thought that I was freed from slavery. Truth be told, I would think this was worse than slavery because I was enslaved in my mind and in bondage to all the horrible things that I had to face.

The nightlife was waiting for me. I was a single black female, smelling good and looking good too and my car was clean, I thought I had it going on. I was dangerous, and this was in a good way. I was not going around being all snooty, but I insisted on holding a private party for my freedom. The dance floor was all mine, and each step that was taken was a step towards victory.

I was looking good in my black jumpsuit on the style of some superhero. I was having a good time taking turns with the guys going to the dance floor. It was amazing how many people could fit on that small dance floor. We loved when the old school mix came on. You could tell when all of the old people were in the house. We started bringing back the old school dance moves like the Electric Slide, Snake, Pee-Wee Herman and please, do not forget the Running Man.

This particular night was strange to me. The Lord has been dealing with me about going out to the clubs, and it seemed so hard for me to let go. Now, when you're single the clubs are one of the hot spots besides church to hang out and try to meet new people. I just want to keep it real for a moment. Now there are some of us that go to the museum, zoo, and bookstore to look for the intellectual type, but typically it's either club or church to find someone that could be a potential mate. When you want to keep it real the majority of us go to either church or a club thinking that we would meet our next love. One of my uncles told me that when you go to the club, you get the club. I will never forget that because in most cases this is a true statement. One thing I have come to learn is that not all people that go to church have the church in them. As my pastor has coined "Everyone that is in the airport isn't going out of town." You have to really be careful. The DJ was up there playing the songs and just talking crazy as usual but again this night was very unusual.

I thought I was the only one up in the club looking cute and you couldn't tell me anything. This one brother offered to buy me a drink, and of course I accepted it. Then that little voice came to my head saying, "Get out of here, this is no place for you." I ignored it, of course, and I'm just stubborn and hard-headed at times. I began to tell this brother about my day and the latest business venture I had going on. He was quite interesting, himself, and had a few irons in the fire. It was ironic that between me sipping on that dark liquor and him drinking beer, we began to talk about the Lord. Some of us have experienced when we get full (and that's full of liquid spirits) things start to come out of our mouths that we forget or don't really mean. Society always says that you will get the truth out of a drunk. We were not at that point yet, so this conversation was truly from the heart. I began to tell him how much of a blessing it was to be in church and how it has changed my life. My expression and my love for God began to come forth in the club.

Subconsciously, I was thinking, 'what a place to talk about the Lord.' Then he began to tell me about his current problems at home with his wife and how he started going to church, and just when he did all hell broke loose around him. He said that his wife had changed and she did not trust him. She did not want to go to church anymore, and so here he was in the club talking to a stranger. The devil is so crafty.

Now, here I am with all my problems explaining to him that we both should not be in the club and that this wasn't the answer to our problems. This was not the way out. He was trying to get some attention from females that he was not getting at that time at home, and I certainly wasn't the one to give it to him. We began to laugh because we knew in our hearts we were not supposed to be there. That was not the end of it because I was hard-headed when that voice spoke to me, and I didn't leave. Still hanging around like I was going to miss something, and soon the DJ started to clown around. Believe it or not, that was one night I can say that God's spirit was in the club. This DJ was raising money to help feed some of the local children that were going without food. In the middle of a song he said, "If I was not a DJ, I would be a preacher. God has been good to us all, so if we can use our money to drink and carry on, why not bless others in our community?" That touched my heart and really confirmed that what this voice was telling me was true, "get out of there."

I do not know how God deals with some of you, but for me, it is in numbers and small revelations. He reveals some but not all things to us. God gives us precise details and tells us calmly what is expected of us. This was the second time that night I should have left the club. Leaving was far from my mind. I wanted to get my ten dollars' worth, and I was trying to feel the effect of my drinks to help aide in all of my drama from this week.

As the night grew, I just was not feeling it. I started to wave my hands instead of snapping my fingers. I began to talk to the Lord internally, and I wasn't attracted to any of the men that I saw. Something was going on here. This was baby-daddy weekend, and I have the house to myself. You do not let a weekend like this go to waste. A few more songs and that was it for me. I decided to head home because there was nothing left for me there and if it was, God blocked it.

Thinking to myself, 'you cannot even go party and not expect the Lord to talk to you." He was all over me, and I could not shake him off even when I was doing things that were displeasing to him. I decided, "You are awesome in all your ways Lord. I give up, and I am going home."

Making my way through the crowd to leave and having foreign men accidentally touch on my body as I maneuvered to the exit door began to disgust me. Finally, I made it through only to see my daughter's community choir director up in the club. I asked him,

"What are you doing here?"

He replied,

"I should be asking you the same thing."

We both laughed as I was leaving out of the club. "See you tomorrow at church," I said. I went to my car shaking my head in amazement. This night was truly weird. Has anyone ever experienced this before? Please let me know. When we start talking about God and witnessing in the club it is time to leave it alone. That day that I am instructed to do so it will be under His direction and I must say, it will be to turn someone around or to pick up a lost soul, or to have clean fun with family and friends. Otherwise, my lesson was learned.

Since it was so late at night and my favorite chicken spot was still open, I decided to join the drive-thru crew and clog up my arteries and eat sloppy bread and hamburger sliced pickles with my chicken.

This was such an evening, and I will never forget it. There was so much for me to digest from this week's events and even what happened at the club. When I got home, I decided that it was in my best interest to take advantage of the few hours of sleep before I went to my scheduled hair appointment. My style lasted for the entire workweek, but after being in the midst of the smoke, the nicotine took over my hair follicles. I only had a few hours before sunrise, and I knew that I had to be on time to the salon.

Day 6:

"The Weekend"

Before I knew it, I was waking up to the alarm on my cell phone to get ready for my hair appointment.

> "My God, I still have not heard from you, and it is morning."

I found myself putting God on my schedule. It was Saturday, and garage sales were calling my name. Unfortunately, this morning the hairdo was first on the agenda, and I could not afford to miss my hair appointment.

While heading up the freeway, I heard this segment from one of the local pastors, and he was talking about how we must forgive those who have persecuted us and have done us wrong. It seems as if forgiveness keeps constantly slapping me in the face. You really think that you have forgiven someone until you have to deal with the issue all over again. We often want people to pay for hurting us but never remember the times that we have hurt someone. Forgiving is the hardest thing to do.

> "I have to do it," I said aloud as I responded back to the pastor on the radio.

It has been a privilege to finally tell my side of the story, and now I cannot seem to get over the forgiving part. No, not me, I must get my crown for all of this misery and hard work. As I walk up the stairs to get my hair done, I see that it was a few of us there on this fine Saturday morning. My ears were filled with laughter, and a few responses of "Amen" as those in attendance engage in shop talk. I came in in the middle of a conversation about how we did not stick together in our black communities.

It was a tendency for clients at the salon to "conversation hop." We would talk about current events and each other's business, and that was okay. It was a form of free therapy if you ask me. It was easy for each of us to join in and talk about our men because each of us brought something different to the table. My stylist did not know that I attended this trial this past week so I thought it would be best that I keep my negative comments about men to myself. Once I was under the dryer, I did not want to add my two cents to the conversation because only negativity would come from my lips and there's no need in sending negative vibes out into the atmosphere.

It took God's Word to set me straight about the experiences that I have had with men. If things would get out of hand, my stylist had a subtle and yet loving way of swaying us back to a more positive conversation.

My respect level for black men decreased, and I felt as though they were at a point of having to prove themselves to me. I love our race, but when it came to relationships, my emotions were in total chaos. This was not a happy-go-lucky situation for me. I did have a mentality of thinking that once a dog, always a dog and I really didn't care anymore because of all the hurt and shame that I was put through. I had to face this hurt and shame alone, and not one of the men that ever abused me took the time to apologize and admit their wrongdoing. The most a man has ever shown me was absolutely nothing, and this is coming from a place that generalize all men that brought negativity and shame to my personal space. They start off a little bit being concerned and then start acting like jerks. The majority of them only wanted to get to know me for that thing that bruised me so easily...sex.

Silly as it sounds and as much literature that is out there I played into the game many times. When will I finally come to my senses? I did not know that my self-worth meant a lot and I had to learn it the hard way. Often enough times it was through break ups that I realized that God had someone else for me. Many times I would try to make things work when God himself was trying to shut them down. I had to go back while under the dryer and ask myself if I was a loser. I seem to attract losers all the time. It seems like my face had this message plastered on it. "I will take the wounded and nurse them back to health only so they can go be with someone else." I believed that my deep desire to be a wife and a mother is what caused me to ignore what I really wanted and accept the potential that I saw in some of these men.

My ability to nurture tends to be my weakness in my relationships. What am I doing? Why do I always seem to be looking for love in all the wrong places? I must know that God loves me and there is not a man out there who could top that. When you fall in love with lust, your mind is confused. You begin to say things you do not mean and want affection that is not worth it. The affections tend to make different emotions turn you into someone you would love to hate. I began to settle, and that was not good. I thought I knew my self-worth, but obviously I still needed some work based on the decisions that I made.

It took years for me to realize that all of this is only a test and it was getting greater and greater. If I could only hold out and see what was planned for me. Sometimes you think you want a particular person in your life only to realize they are not good enough for you and they were not God's choice, but yours. It is not to say that you think that you are all that and a bag of chips and that person is not a good person, it's only to confirm that their goodness isn't what God ordered for you.

There is not a price that you can put on "old mother wit," better known as old wisdom. That is usually administered from one of the ladies that just finished a press and curl or roller set. They can tell you everything about how to keep your man, right down to how to pick greens. It was my time to sit in the hot seat. Today I did not have a topic because there was a lot on my mind already, and sharing my week's events was not a topic of discussion to the clients in the salon. We were already heated with thoughts and loads of deception. I did not need to kill the excitement with my story. Who was interested in me anyway or what I had to say? This was just my weekend of healing. Why not start with a fresh hairdo? My outer appearance was just as important as the inner me. I learned so much on that morning. There was not anything else that could be added to the topic of discussion today. Once in the stylist chair, my opinions didn't even matter. My body was in the seat, but my mind was on the other side of town.

This day I took my pastor's advice and decided that once I was done, I would take myself out to lunch. Since it was an ongoing goal of mine to run into "Mr. Right," I figured it might be a good idea to learn how to treat myself better. I never went to a movie by myself or even took myself to a restaurant. That was very critical for me to learn how to love myself more than me requesting a man to give me all of him. I need to learn how to first treat me well before I put this burden on someone else.

I left the salon deciding that I would treat myself to seafood. This was a very awkward feeling for me. How do you tell the hostess that it would be just one in your party? The first thing they assume is that you want to go to the bar. Well, I had to overcome this fear of doing things alone. Now, do not get me wrong. I can shop by myself but going on a date with me, myself, and I, el numero uno... *that* was *absurd*!

While this wasn't easy for me, I knew it was a fear that must be conquered once and for all. I would look at the families and couples pass by and then get discouraged and want to just crawl up like Charlie Brown and whomp, whomp, whomp right out of the restaurant. When it was time to order it was difficult to make it through without crying. Although it was difficult, it had to be done. I took this opportunity to be nice to myself. I even turned the cell phone off so I can experience that alone time. Did I really like myself? Can I treat myself as well as I expect others to treat me?

When my food came, I was not even hungry. It was a chore trying to eat without wanting to just leave with a to-go-box in hand. This taught me a valuable lesson. I need to do this more often. This time was well deserved and much needed, and I can appreciate the alone time.

The rest of the evening was mine, and I really did not know what to do with it. Since I had already gone to the club the night before, what else could a girl get into? I figured that this weekend was not for girlfriends. We love people, but solitude is highly suggested every now and then. Going to the movie was out of the question. I was not going to waste my money and fall asleep on the movie as I normally do. Our collection of movies allowed me to save money, be entertained, and fall asleep all in the privacy of my own home. Chick flicks were out of the question. I did not want to get mad about men or sob with a box of Kleenex nearby. Scary movies and pure action were out of the question as well because I didn't need any subliminal influences to act as triggers to take me back to wanting to harm my predators. This was time for me to get it together.

I decided to drift towards one of my greatest escapes, music! A little smooth jazz is definitely the start of a nice quiet evening. I was able to burn some candles that I reserved for a special occasion, and tonight was special to me. This was the birthing of a new me and in turn I must celebrate. I challenged myself earlier to do something that I was not accustomed to doing, taking myself out on a date. Out with the old and in with the new and improved was my new mindset.

My mind was set on listening to jazz, but that voice within me sent me to the tapes from church that I had borrowed from one of my church sisters. This sister was very loving and was willing to let me borrow some cassette tapes to comfort my spirit when I was going through some things. I would listen in my car and at night before I went to sleep but this was Saturday evening, and the sun had not gone down yet. I put this one tape in, and it was talking about love. Have you ever thought of your life as being a permanent set up? The tapes that they gave me were very old, but the message was new to me. It was very well needed at this time in my life. I listened to this tape repeatedly, and each time I would dissect and stop it periodically to try to find how the message applied to my current situation. When it was brought to my attention the message was not hidden, it was very much alive for my spirit. I said I loved God, but it was hard for me to love those who were not there for me. Never did it occur to me until now, that this is all a part of the plan.

God's purpose for my life was for the hurts and tribulation that I experienced to one day bring honor and glory to him. Energy was flowing all through my house. My temple was filled with so many uncertainties and negativity. Yes, I was positive and could give you encouragement, but behind closed doors it was different. I had to overcome a few monsters called fear, doubt, and disbelief. You can say that you trust the Lord, but do you really *trust* Him?

Do you really depend on Him to be the head of your life *totally*? Do you give Him bits and pieces of those things that you want him to fix instantly? Do you give Him your finances without giving Him your relationships? Do you give him your physical attacks and leave your negative thoughts of impure motives lingering in your mind? We all do it. We treat God just like the next best deal when comparison shopping. We go down the aisle trying to find a bargain, and all discounts aren't of quality.

All my life I was trying to bargain with God and He was there all the time. In the stores, you usually find out that the generic is just as good as the name brands and the manufacturers of the brand products are some way connected with the generic. I said all of that to say that God is there with us no matter what the situation may be. He confirmed in his word that he will never forsake us. Some of us have been tossed about like a sailboat that is just riding the waves and some of us have also experienced a sinking situation. It is during these times that we need to remember that God is with us all the time. Some of the difficult times in life are for us to see that with God our survival skills are demonstrated at their best. This is a time when we learn that there is someone higher than us that will allow us and teach us how to stay afloat.

God allows us to go through these types of experiences so that we can find more than the good in our lives, but the God in our lives. Through some of these experiences, we learn that what is good *to* us is not always good *for* us. Looking for God in your life is *godly*. Godliness is a good character trait that we should all develop until it becomes second nature in our lives. As I looked for God, I realized that He had another plan for me this evening, and I was rather enjoying it. This time I could hear Him. We just chilled out. I prayed and talked to him. Our conversation was two- way and I could hear Him this time. I did not just make my requests known, but I also listened for a response.

When we just talk to him and never allow our ears to listen to the sender's message, we could miss what he is trying to tell us. God is always trying to get our attention. He is so good to us that he makes us aware of things, but often we are too busy in our thought process that we miss the message. When we miss our personal message from him, we tend to become confused about what had most recently occurred.

This was another one of those nights where I fell asleep while conversing with God. It was early Sunday morning about 3:00 a.m. when I finally woke up from drifting to sleep. My heart soon whispered a name, as if it was waiting for me to wake up. My heart knew that we had some work to do. Do you remember the word that was discussed earlier about forgiveness? This was the time to wipe the slate clean and get on with my life. This was the work that I needed to complete.

When you ask your Father to use you, He will do just that. Before He does, however, there is a molding process. When you think that you are the finest of the finest crystal on the shelf, you're really not. Yes, you are pretty on the outside, and you stand out, but you are subject to chip or break and need some repair. Someone during your lifetime will do just that; chip you or try to break you, that pretty piece of crystal. It is usually when the crystal is moved from shelf to shelf or from place to place that it becomes fragile or broken. God will allow you to get chipped or broken so He can restore you as the fine piece of stemware that only He can fix.

There is nothing too hard for God. I never thought that God would use someone like me to pray for others. This latest list of people was comprised of relatives, friends, and acquaintances. I had to forgive them so that I too could be forgiven. I had actually forgotten about some of the people that came to mind. Evidently, I had not forgotten about them totally because my Spirit led me to pray for them. God even had me to pray and forgive this one man who took my life savings! Friends, enemies, family, acquaintances...all were on my to-do list for the day. Yes, this day God had planned some real work for me; and although my week was tough, this day was most important that I not call-in sick.

Day 7:

"Words of Wisdom"

While I was up praying for others, God took me down memory lane. I was able to reflect on different situations and how God delivered me from them all. The time was growing later in the morning, and our first church services started at 7:30 a.m. I did not want to miss this service and to yawn in service would have been rude. Immediately I began asking for strength to make it to church on time.

I was able to make church service despite the long night I had praying and talking to the Father. I stepped through the doors expecting a specific Word from God. I just knew that I would receive encouragement to keep moving forward. The pastor's message this morning was about the prodigal son. We were reminded that we are children of the Most-High God. We belong to a mighty God, and no matter what storms come in our lives, we must remember who we are. These last seven days of my life helped me to realize what I have reiterated almost every day. Pushing past my pain to fulfill my purpose is not about me. It is more than me. The bigger picture is filled with more people. If only I knew what was on the other side of my story. I may not know the exact outcome, but I know it's for God's glory.

Seven days of healing was to reach some boy, girl, man or woman that has suffered from abuse. I can relate to sexual abuse that also entailed verbal and emotional abuse. When the devil tries to take you out when you're young, please know that you are *destined to be successful*. Does success mean that you are going to be rich? No, it does not. It means that you are going to be *wealthy*!

The definition of wealthy is "richly supplied." Once this understanding was deeply embedded in my Spirit, it helped me to see that I would always have abundance. This means everything from knowledge to material goods as well. Wisdom and peace are priceless, and an overflow is available for us to share with others. God had begun to show me that I was going to be a wealthy woman. With my carnal mind, I was looking for some get-rich-quick scheme or someone in the family winning the lotto and giving me a portion. When I saw that God would take what He blessed me with to bless others, then that was enough to make me feel enriched with His God-given love.

The devil has been after me since I was a toddler. He was allowed to take me on a ride that was supposed to kill me. The negative thoughts often made me want to kill myself. I believe that God allowed him to continue to test me over and over again. I could be wrong about this statement, but I honestly believe some of us are made to go through the fire. Once we come out of the fire, we can then tell others about who it was that got us through without obtaining any burn marks or bruises.

God has been making me stronger and stronger after each obstacle course that I overcome. The strength wasn't only for me; it was for some of you. I wrote this book to tell my story so that you can get to know God on an intimate level. Some of you need to know that God loves you no matter what obstacle you may be struggling with. Maybe you were introduced to sex at an early age, or someone threatened to kill you if you didn't participate. In either case I believe that God loves you and still wants the best from you. Do not believe the hype or the lies that God do not love you because of your sin? God loves you despite your sin – so much so, that he sent his Son to die for you *because* of sin. God doesn't like sin, but ***he is madly in love with you!***

The Beginning of a New You
God has got you right in his hand. I encourage you not to allow what has entrapped you for such a long time continue to take control over you. Sure, people may have taken your virginity but do not allow that incident to take away your dignity. God is a restorer and will restore you back on the path that was originally meant for you if you would only take out the time to ask him for help!

Please do not send out the death wish for people that did you wrong. Let God handle it. This is something that I had to learn the hard way. I had so much hatred and premeditated thoughts in my mind, and there was nothing godly about it. What was meant to hurt you may turn out to bless you. It is certainly a blessing for me to share my story with total strangers. This was not some stunt for me but a requirement from God. Many of our children are being molested, and many predators are popping up on the scene daily. Some of us have become so involved with making a living that we allow our children to fend for themselves. We have to get back to raising our children by being more involved in their lives and not allow technology to replace our values and concepts of parenting.

I speak to you just as I speak to myself. Just recently, I received a personal message from God to stop and raise my children. I worked all my life trying to chase a dollar to survive - so much so that my little one's lives were passing me by. It is time that we have real, authentic conversations with our children about sex, but with tact and respect and the long list of consequences. The world is ready to show and tell them something contrary to what you teach at home. Our children are brilliant, and we have to be honest and convey to them in whatever creative and imaginative way possible the truth about sex. We also have to protect our children and let them know what is and is not permissible. We have to make sure that they know that our door is open to them and that we are here for them. We must encourage them to not be afraid to tell us what is going on in their lives. We have to enforce that encouragement with right reactions when they do open up and share. We have to be ready to share some of our own personal experiences with them so that they can know that they are not strange and that we can relate to their experiences.

I strongly recommend therapy when dealing with sexual abuse. Therapists are trained to help us to get over the humps and continue on with life. However, God will listen when your therapist's office is closed. Developing that personal relationship with God is so important, and seeking a Christian counselor or therapists would be icing on the cake. I am not suggesting that you do not continue on with your current sessions or to use God as an alternative, I am only sharing how I got through some of the most difficult times of my life. I am so happy that God chose me for this.

It is like a domino effect, what he can do for one of us he can do for us all. I love each and every one of you that God is going to allow to read this book and relate my situation to anything that may be holding you back in life. You can do whatever it is that God has purposed for you to do. Let us all that have been trapped by negativity, sex, drugs, alcohol, abuse, and fear to say no more and start with ourselves first and then reach out to our communities and make this world a better place to live.

This next line may not get that much recognition. Predators out there, God loves you, too. You must stop allowing the enemy to use you in destroying other people's lives. Know that God can change you, too, because the ones that you've hurt were defenseless.

Mothers, teach your children at an early age to recognize the enemy. The enemy usually uses those who are close to us to hurt us and that's only because we are trusting. A potential predator statistically, is one that knows the child well. It could be a friend of the family or even a relative. This day and time we hear of more teachers and public authority figures that have crossed the line with our children. We are taught to obey and trust those in authority. Unfortunately, those who are in authority can misuse their power and tamper with an innocent soul.

We have power, and it begins with our speech. We can either speak life or death. Which one do you prefer; life or death? We must teach our children the power of their words. We must teach them to say, "Devil, I recognize you, and you are not welcomed here." I believe if this one statement is spoken aloud or inwardly during our most challenging times, it will put a stop to the enemy and his evil forces from having a long term effect in our lives.

My advice that I give to parents is to know your children. In today's times, we do not fully know our children. Sending them to school and occasionally having family outings and church does not constitute knowing your child. Will your child tell you everything? No, that is impossible. It is fine to get downright raunchy with them at times to get the point across. They are yours. If you do not tell them the right way of doing things and communicate with them on a level that they may understand, then strangers will take the opportunity to give them their version of truth. We do not know every evil thought or force that is waiting to destroy our children. All we can do is utilize the time and tools we have been given and talk to them in a way that they can understand. Personally, I have "rap sessions" with my children regularly to teach them on how to be aware of the enemy and his tactics.

I am not a family guidance counselor, but the assignment that the Lord has given me is to share my story, and if it only saves or changes one person's life, my work is complete. We must let our children be aware of those who are close to them.

We must fight to make sure that if we were victims in the past that the hurt is dealt with until it is gone and we are now victors. As God's creation across the globe, we have the power to make changes and help one another to get the job done. It is our duty to defeat shame and allow healing within ourselves and know that God is in control of it all. Can we make a difference? Sure, we can and we will. Let us stand in the gap for one another and put a stop to sexual abuse, mental and verbal abuse, domestic violence and any other means of self-destruction. The beginning of an end is the best beginning we can experience because that shows a sign of healing. Receive your healing today and be blessed. No more heartache and pain will dwell in your house.

My prayer is that every person that reads this book would obtain a new beginning in your life, and that all that you do be to the glory and honor of our God above.

I ask the Lord to heal you inwardly and outwardly and restore you to his original purpose before your life was interrupted. I pray that the Lord keep you as you grow stronger in the understanding that God loves you – no matter what. Amen!

About the Author

Rochelle Washington is a graduate from Dallas Baptist University located in Dallas, TX. Rochelle is a Communications Major that loves to couple her creativity with her gifts to communicate with the world. Because of her passion to encourage and inspire, Rochelle leveraged her passion for the advancement of women and turned her passion into a business. Rochelle Washington is the CEO of Bold, Beautiful & Blessed, a brand that is dedicated to empower and inspire women across the globe.

In her spare time, Rochelle loves creative writing, dancing, and spending time with her family. You can reach Rochelle Washington by visiting www.boldbeautifulblessed.com or email at boldbeautifulblessed1@gmail.com.

Credits:

Edit, Layout, and Publishing services provided by
Nurisha Liggins for GLOW Publications
Twitter/IG: @iAmNurisha

Art Director and Graphic Designer
Art Direction and Cover Design by Gannon Crutcher –
Cnytexan227@aol.com, IG and FB: gannontheartist